SEEING
THE BIBLE
WHOLE

Daily Bible readings
and notes

SEEING
THE BIBLE
WHOLE

by
Stephen Neill

Published by
THE BIBLE READING FELLOWSHIP
St. Michael's House
2 Elizabeth St, London SW1

© BRF 1977

First published 1957
Fourth impression 1970
New edition (re-set) 1977

SBN 900164 40 9

Printed and Bound in Great Britain by
Hazell Watson & Viney Ltd, Aylesbury, Bucks

CONTENTS

To the reader   1
General Introduction   3

FIRST MONTH
The beginning and the end   9
The prophets   15
Prophecy and history   38

SECOND MONTH
The kingdom   50
Captivity and return   61
The end of the Old Testament   70
The inner life of a people   77
Between Old and New   89

THIRD MONTH
The life of the Master   92

FOURTH MONTH
Working it out   125
Thinking it through   132
Later books of the New Testament   144

Old Testament Chronology   14
The New Testament   90
The New Testament (2)   123
Some Prayers   159
Index   160

Many things in the world have changed since *Seeing the Bible Whole* was first written. During these years the Christian faith has been exposed to venomous and ruthless assaults carried out by enemies of many different kinds. There has been a great increase in secularism, and many find it difficult to believe in anything they cannot measure and number and weigh. But now a change seems to be on the way. Those who have followed these various modern nostrums, most of which have this in common, that they are entirely negative as to the existence of any unseen world, have found that the way in which they were walking led nowhere but to a brick wall. It is the work of the Bible to open a door in that brick wall, and to reveal the wonderful world which lies beyond it. Some of those who go through the door are likely to find themselves dazzled by the brilliance of the light and by the rich variety of the objects that they encounter. For such, and for others, this little book is written, to help them through the period until their eyes get adjusted and they begin to feel themselves at home in this brave new world.

The notes are printed roughly in the chronological order, taking the Old Testament first. This is perhaps the logical way of going about it. First things first. But to some people 'first' means 'most important'; they prefer to plunge straight into the heart of things in the New Testament and to encounter directly the challenge of Jesus Christ. This also is a perfectly sensible way of proceeding. If any readers prefer to take the months in the order 3, 4, 1, 2, they may find this method of study fits in best with their way of getting at things. But, wherever readers start, the important thing is that they should all end up in the same place. So these pages are sent out again, for the fifth time, with my good wishes to all readers and in the hope that they may make the great discovery that the Bible really does make sense of things.

The Bible is a very big book and a very perplexing one. We are always told that it is the Word of God, and that we shall find God in it. But how many people have started off hopefully at the beginning, expecting to meet with God, have become hopelessly lost somewhere about Leviticus, and have then read no more. This may have been the experience of some who are now setting out to 'see the Bible as a whole'.

If we are to read the Bible with any profit, the first condition is to remember that it is a collection of writings the origin of which is spread over an immensely long period of time. The oldest passage which we can date with approximate certainty is the Song of Deborah (Judges 5), which belongs to the 12th century BC. The latest book of the Bible is probably 2 Peter, which was written in the first half of the 2nd century AD. Thirteen centuries is a very long time; if we think in terms of English history, we shall be carried back to the 600s, that is far beyond 1066 and all that, beyond even the time of Alfred the Great, almost as far back as the mission of Augustine to Canterbury in AD 597.

Moreover, these writings are most varied in their character. We shall find primitive tales and carefully elaborated histories, poems and ancient proverbial sayings, parables and orations, ethical instruction and deep philosophical musings, prophecy and allegory and vision. Not all of this material is of equal value. Much of it speaks to us directly today, as it has to men of every age and race. Other parts we can see to have been of great value to men at a different stage of development from our own, yet may doubt their significance for ourselves. Of some parts we may wonder why they find a place in the Bible at all.

The Bible is not a tidy book. It is all drawn directly from life, and is no tidier than life itself. Yet, if we are patient with it, we may begin to see a pattern and a plan emerging, just as those of us who read the daily papers may begin to see a pattern of great movements emerging from the confusion of our times, and just as those of us who have reached middle age, looking back over our lives, may begin to recognise a plan developing through what at the time seemed merely chance events.

The Bible is all about God. He comes in the first verse—'In the beginning God'; on the last page he speaks of himself in the solemn formula 'I am the Alpha and the Omega, the beginning and the end.'

But this is not just any kind of God; he is a very particular kind of God, and, though at times very imperfectly known by men, always the same kind of God; it is the unity of his nature and his purpose that makes up the unity of the Bible.

First, he is a God who acts, and history is the sphere of his activity. Again and again, we read that God spoke, God made, God saw, God loved, God came, God saved.

Secondly, he is a God whose action always moves forward from the smaller to the larger. He is concerned with the whole universe and with all peoples; but he chooses one people in which specially to reveal himself, in order that through that one people blessing may come to all. In the Church, he is acting in exactly the same way today.

Thirdly, he is a patient God, who is apparently willing to allow his plans to be for a long time frustrated by man's misuse of the liberty that he himself has given. The story of the Bible goes on through long periods in which apparently nothing of importance happens, and through epochs of disaster in which everything appears to go clean contrary to God's will. And still the plan is there, and moves on towards that fulfilment which is certain, because God himself is pledged to bring it about.

Fourthly, he is a God who invites. He brings his plans to fruition only through the co-operation of men whom he has called. But their cooperation must be free, voluntary and joyful. The name by which this co-operation is known in the Bible is 'faith'.

Fifthly, he is a God who confirms in experience the reality of his calling. The Bible is not simply a record of things that happened long ago. It deals with living experiences into which we can enter today. We may take our stand with Abraham and Moses and Elijah, and with the Christ himself. As we so take our stand, we discover for ourselves that the words they said, and the things that are written about them, are true.

Finally, God is a God who promises. The whole movement of the Bible is forward to a consummation that is not yet revealed, though hints of its nature are given. We are called to run the same race as the great men of old, 'God having provided some better thing concern-us, that apart from us they should not be made perfect' (Hebrews 11:40).

We ought by now to have some idea of the way in which we ought to approach the Bible, and the spirit in which we ought to read.

1. We must read *patiently.* It takes time to accustom ourselves to the language of the Bible and to the climate of its thought. This is true even if we abandon the classical Authorised Version of 1611 and read a modern version. The trouble is that the great words which must be

used in any version of the Bible—words like 'grace' and 'light' and 'love'—have got so worn away in our modern usage that it takes time before we can grasp what they meant when they were new-minted words, carrying full value in the commerce of thought. Just the same process of 'learning the language' has to be gone through in becoming familiar with any great writer—Shakespeare, Milton, Browning; and perhaps on this level the demands made by the Bible are less than those made on their readers by such recent writers as T. S. Eliot or Christopher Fry.

2. We must read *sympathetically*. The writers of the Bible differ greatly among themselves; but in essentials they all share a common point of view—a sense of being confronted by a living God at work in his world. It is not a question, at the moment, of whether we accept this point of view and believe what the writers of the Bible believed. It is just that we shall not be able to understand what they are talking about, unless as we read we put ourselves, at least for the time being, at the point from which they are looking out upon the world. This has been well put by Professor Paul Minear. Speaking of pictures, he says that what unifies a picture is 'the point at which the artist stands. Unless the onlooker stands at that centre he does not see the painting as the artist sees it. If there is to be communication, the onlooker need not share the painter's views but he must share the painter's *point of viewing*. He need not agree with his *standpoint*, but he must *stand* at the same *point*' (*Eyes of Faith*, p. 1).

3. We must read *with imagination*. We must not stop to let ourselves be perplexed by the first difficulty that encounters us in our reading. We are told that what was written of old-time was written *for our learning* (Romans 15:4); we are not told that it was all written for our example! We need not be surprised to find that men of a much earlier day acted in a way that would be shocking in those who have received the Gospel of Christ. We may find ourselves wondering whether all the marvels recorded in the Old Testament are true. That is certainly a question on which, at a later stage, we shall have to make up our minds. For the moment, let us be content to read the words in the spirit in which they were written, and as far as possible through the minds of those to whom they originally came.

4. We must read *with humility*. It is unlikely that each day's reading will bring to us a clear and decisive message from God. There may well be moments at which we are tempted to give up our reading. At such moments, it may be well to remember that even the latest parts of the Bible have been 'Holy Scripture', the Word of God, for more than sixty generations. If we do not find them so ourselves, it is at least possible that the fault is in ourselves, and not in what we read.

5

All great writing is to be approached with reverence, and with a sense of unworthiness. Who are we that the secrets of all the ages should be unlocked for us? And yet the promise is that, if we draw near in the right spirit of humility, that is exactly what will happen.

Even when we have fulfilled all the necessary conditions of approach, the question of the order in which we should arrange our reading of the Bible still remains to be faced.

There is quite a lot to be said for starting with the New Testament. This is, after all, by far the most important part of the Bible, and this is the method that is naturally followed in instructing those of other faiths who wish to join the Church. But the Old Testament does come before the New. Our Lord and the Apostles built on the faith that they found set forth in it. Perhaps it will be good to look first at the Jewish foundations before we come on to consider the Christian super-structure.

If we start with the Old Testament, the most natural course would seem to be to follow the order of the books as they are printed in the English Bible. That is the Bible most readers will use all their lives, though everyone knows that the books are not printed in the order in which they were originally written.

But in the end the decision has been made to start with the great writing prophets of the Old Testament. Though this part of the Bible is not in genral well known even to regular churchgoers, it does in fact contain the heart of the Old Testament message. Each prophet is a character in his own right, whom we can come to know through study of his writings. These prophets stand in the full light of history. They are almost contemporary with such other great movements of human thought as the early philosophers in Greece, the early Upanishads in India, and Confucius in China. Their words are spoken in relation to events which are attested also in those records of Assyria and Babylonia that scholars can now read and understand.

Moreover, the prophets look both backwards and forwards; and, standing at the vantage point of their proclamation, we can do the same. They were always recalling to the people the story of God's great actions in the past, and the whole earlier history came to be rewritten in the light of the profound prophetic musing upon the meaning of history and of God's purposes in it.

And they looked forward to a future fulfilment of those purposes, which we can see in part to have come about in Christ, but part of which is future even to us, since there is still an end and a consum-mation of God's purposes which to us also is the object of hope and not yet of experience.

We shall start, then, by making some encounter with the great prophets, as they challenge the people to a direct meeting with the living God who draws near to them in his word. We shall then take a rapid glance at the history of the Jewish nation over more than a thousand years, in its various stages of call, preparation, splendour, decline, disaster, captivity and renewal. The last part of our Old Testament study will deal with the inner life of the people as that expressed itself in worship, in aspiration, in deeper thought upon the problems of the universe.

Then, at the end of two months, we shall be ready to turn to the New Testament. And here again we meet at once a problem as to the order in which the books should be read.

Many Christians do not realise that, historically, the Epistles come before the Gospels. All the Epistles of St Paul, and perhaps some of the others as well, were written before the first Gospel appeared. The Churches which received the written Gospels were Churches which had already lived and suffered and witnessed for a generation, and in that period had striven to work out the full meaning of their faith in Christ. It might seem natural to follow the historical order of writing—first to meet the Churches engaged in the fight of faith, and then to go back to the records of the Christ in whom they had believed.

But here the decision has gone the other way. What the earliest Christians had been taught by word of mouth had been roughly the contents of our present Gospels, especially the stories of the Passion and Resurrection of Christ. That was the basis of their faith, and without that preaching there would have been no Churches at all. We cannot recover that stage of oral preaching; but it has seemed best to start with the life of Jesus, as given in the first three Gospels, and then to go on to the Epistles to study the experience of the Churches that were trying to live by the Gospel and to work out its full meaning The Fourth Gospel, which is later than the other three, is mostly kept over to this section, to be studied as part of the working out of the meaning of the Gospel.

The extracts chosen for reading can give only a fragmentary picture of the riches of the Bible—not more than a twentieth of the whole can be included in four months' readings. The reader will note that, on a good many days, a longer reading is indicated in brackets; if time permits he is most strongly recommended to take the longer selection, though not at the expense of careful reading. But naturally this four months' course of readings is put out in the hope that at the end the reader may find himself impelled to launch out boldly for himself on the shoreless sea of divine wisdom that is to be found in the Holy Scriptures of the Old and New Testaments.

So now we are ready to begin, and to open the Bible itself. But, before we tackle the prophets, we shall take a rapid glance at the beginning of the story; and then, contrary to what is recommended for the reader of detective stories, we shall leap forward to the last pages, and take a glance at them. These first four readings will give us an idea of what the story is all about, and of the direction in which we are moving. To use a clumsy modern expression, they will serve as 'orientation' for the whole of the rest of our reading.

THE BEGINNING AND THE END

☐ Genesis was not the first book of the Bible to be written, and Revelation was probably not the last. But, from a time long before the birth of Jesus, Genesis has stood at the beginning of the Old Testament; and from a very early period of the history of the Church, Revelation has stood at the end of the New. We may think that there was a kind of inspiration also in this arrangement of the books.

The first three and the last three chapters of the Bible lay down for us certain principles in the relationship between God and his world which we may summarise as follows:

1. God made the whole universe, and is in control of every single part of it. *2.* God made his universe good; he delights in it and loves it. *3.* Since evil has entered in, through the freedom that God himself had given to man, the world is not in the state in which God intended it to be. *4.* God is all the time at work to overcome evil, and to bring men and the world back to himself. *5.* In the end, evil will be wholly cast out, and God's good purpose will be perfectly fulfilled.

The beginning and the end of the Bible are like two pillars on which the whole structure rests, and there is a remarkable correspondence between them. Here we have the creation of the heavens and the earth, there new heavens and a new earth. Here evil enters in; there, into that other, nothing that defiles shall enter in. Here man is consigned to death; there they shall reign for ever and ever. Here, the visible presence of God is withdrawn from men; there 'his servants shall serve him; and they shall see his face.'

A careful study of these, and the other great ideas in these chapters will be an invaluable initiation into the vocabulary of the Bible, and into its way of thinking.

FIRST MONTH

HOW IT ALL BEGAN

Genesis 1, vv. 1 to 8; 1, v. 26 to 2, v. 4(1, v. 1 to 2, v. 4,)

The Greeks, for all their wonderful cleverness, never arrived at the idea of creation. Sometimes they thought of God as imposing form on matter which already existed and which was never completely responsive to his will; sometimes they thought of God as it were extending himself in space, so that the universe was a kind of emanation of his being. The unphilosophical Jews went straight to the idea of creation. How did the world come into being? God made it. How did he make it? By his word. What did he make it out of? Out of nothing. First, there was just God; then there was God and the universe.

A great deal of ink has been spilt in trying to reconcile Genesis 1 with scientific discovery. It is, indeed, remarkable that there is so little in this very ancient poem that is contrary to modern science. But that is not the point. To the Hebrew writer, this was not a question of science or philosophy; it was a religious question—what is the relationship between God and the world? The answer is that he is absolutely Lord over it all; he cares for it and rules over it, and nothing in it can ever pass beyond his control: 'In his hand are all the corners of the earth' (Psalm 95:4).

If we ask '*Why* did God create the universe?' we cannot find an answer to our question; and yet perhaps we can come near to a true answer. We know nothing, ourselves, of creation out of nothing: we can only work on what already exists. But the artist, and specially the musician, sometimes comes very near to pure creation; and we find that man is at his happiest, when he is making or creating something. It may be that creation, and the care of created things, is part of the happiness of God himself.

To think over *It has been said that more Hindus have been converted to Christianity through reading the first three chapters of Genesis than through anything else. Can you see why this might be so?*

Genesis 3, vv. 1 to 24 (2, v. 5 to 3, v. 24)

God saw that the world he had made was very good (1:31); and yet it is clear that large parts of it are not all good. What has happened?

Genesis 3 is a splendid instance of the way in which the Bible takes an old, old story, and turns it into a vehicle to convey profound spiritual truth. The figures of a man and a woman and a serpent by a tree can be seen in any book of pictures of Babylonian and Assyrian monuments. What has Genesis made of this old tale? This is not a philosophical discourse on the nature of evil—it is a marvellously acute analysis of the nature of evil as we find it in ourselves, and as we see it developing in our children. Here are the main points:

1. Evil comes into existence only as a function of human freedom. 2. It can be recognised as such only in relation to a *commandment*, a standard external to ourselves which we accept as valid (v. 3). 3. The existence of the commandment brings with it the frightful possibility that it might be disobeyed (v. 1). 4. Temptation is not sin, but temptation usually takes the form of specious argument to prove that wrong is right (vv. 4–5). 5. Wrong action is not immediately followed by any disastrous consequence. 6. The wrongdoer usually likes to have a partner in wrongdoing—how else would evil be propagated in the world? (v. 6). 7. The result of exposure is that peculiarly human emotion—shame (vv. 8–11). 8. Exposure almost invariably is followed by the desire to make excuse—to put the blame on someone else—a tendency much encouraged by psychiatrists at the present time (vv. 12–13). 9. Wrongdoing always results in division—man is divided against himself; he is set against his brother (4:1–15); he is deprived of immediate fellowship with God (vv. 22–24).

Genesis 3 is not often quoted in the rest of the Bible; but the whole story is that of God's strategy in overcoming evil, and of his final victory over it.

To think over *'As in Adam all die, so also in Christ shall all be made alive' (I Corinthians 15 v. 22 ; and read 15 vv. 20 to 26).*

Revelation 21, vv. 1 to 12 (21, vv. 1 to 27)

The Book of Revelation, written in a time of bitter persecution for the Church, is full of the sound of conflict and war. In the Bible the power of man, organised in independence of God or in defiance of his will, is seen under the form of a succession of great cities, of which the last is Babylon (Rome—the sum total of human rebellion against God). It is only when Babylon is at last overthrown that we can be brought to the peaceful vision of the new heavens and the new earth. Clearly these last two chapters of the Bible are written as a pendent to the story of the Creation and the Fall which we read in Genesis; here we find the reversal of the curse, and the fulfilment of the purpose. Anyone who reads these chapters with the help of a reference Bible will find that almost every one of the great Old Testament symbols comes back here, often in a new and glorified form.

Three points specially concern us:

1. Here the living presence of God is restored to man. In the Old Testament the temple at Jerusalem was the sign of God's presence, and at its dedication was filled with his glory. But that was only a symbol. Now there is no need for symbol or sacrament, since the faithful shall have the very reality of God's presence. That is why we celebrate the Holy Communion only 'until his coming again'.

2. There is no false otherworldliness in the Bible. The promise is only 'to him that overcometh'. To overcome is to accept without dismay the evil, the strife and the apparently meaningless suffering that are the lot of men in this life, to serve with patience, to bear witness courageously to the truth and if necessary suffer for it. The Church is not primarily a hospital for the infirm; it is a place of discipline for those who are willing to be made strong.

3. The golden age of Christianity is not in the past but in the future. History is not meaningless; it begins in a garden, but it ends in a city, the true Jerusalem. And 'city' in this sense speaks of a divine ordering and pattern for man's life, a joyful obedience of man to God, and unlimited service of man to man. Wherever on earth these three ideals are in part realised, there is a foretaste of the true and heavenly city.

Revelation 22, vv. 1 to 21

In our human life good and evil are inextricably mixed up together, and we cannot separate them. God has allowed this, but he cannot allow it for ever. Good has within it the nature of permanence; evil is self-destructive, and in the end it must be destroyed. In this passage we have a picture of the final separation. Everything that is good has been gathered into the city of God (v. 3); everything that is evil is forever outside (v. 15).

The passage makes it clear that whether a man is inside or outside depends in the last resort on his own choice. The blessedness of those who are in the city is that now their wills are for ever and un-changeably fixed on God and cannot turn away from him; this is the true freedom of man, which here we can only imperfectly enjoy. The New Testament will not let us evade the possibility that a man might go on so long rebelling against God that in the end he might not be able to change. So for him too there would be a 'for ever'—for ever fixed in rebellion against God.

This picture of the future makes sense to us, in spite of its highly picturesque language, because it depicts only the fulness of some-thing that we already know in part. In this life we do see God in the face of Jesus Christ; here we do serve him, though very imperfectly; here we are refreshed by the waters of the river of life. 'F. D. Maurice is surely right in refusing to treat this vision as being but a glimpse into the future. The New Testament writers ... rested their hopes upon the realities of the past and the actualities of the present. Their eager anticipation of things to come was an *a fortiori* argument from the good already experienced, not a compensation' (M. A. C. Warren). Here our experience is fitful and inconstant; there it will be steady and complete in the light of one unchanging eternity.

Prayer *O Almighty God, who hast knit together thine elect in one communion and fellow-ship in the mystical body of thy Son Christ our Lord ; Grant us grace so to follow thy blessed Saints in all virtuous and godly living, that we may come to those unspeakable joys, which thou hast prepared for them that unfeignedly love thee; through Jesus Christ our Lord.* Amen.

Nearly all English Bibles at one time had in the margins Archbishop Ussher's Chronology, worked out in the 17th century. Many of Ussher's dates are now known to have been inaccurate; but on the whole the provision of such aids was a good thing, as the reader at least knew in what century the events he was reading about were supposed to have taken place.

Ussher started with the Creation in 4004 BC. This was a ridiculous date for the Creation; but, oddly enough, Ussher's date is roughly correct for the beginning of *civilised* man—man who records his thoughts in writing and can pass them on to others. Scholars have traced history back, both in Egypt and Babylonia, to about 4000 BC, and perhaps a little further. But it is very unlikely that any written document we have today is as much as 6,000 years old.

About halfway between the birth of civilisation and the birth of Christ comes the birth of the Jewish nation, with the call of Abraham. So, very roughly indeed, we have three great periods:

4000–2000	Before Abraham
2000–0	Abraham to Christ
0–19**	Christ to the present day

Taking the history of Israel, we can divide it again very roughly into periods of four hundred years:

1800–1400	Abraham to the Exodus: Israel in Egypt (but many scholars would put the Exodus nearly two hundred years later)
1400–1000	The Conquest of Canaan, the Judges and the Early Kingdoms
1000–600	The Kingdoms of Israel and Judah
600–200	Israel in Captivity and under foreign rulers.

This covers almost the whole of the period in which the Old Testament was being written; Daniel and some Psalms may be later than 200 BC.

Now to come a little closer, and to look at the actual books of the Old Testament in their historical setting.

Comparatively few events can be dated with perfect accuracy, but we can say with some certainty that in 1000 BC David was King. A few parts of the Old Testament are older than the time of David, especially some of the ancient poems; but it may be taken as certain that no complete book existed at that date. Now let us indicate the main periods of Jewish history, and the contribution which each made to the growth of the Old Testament as we have it.

c. 1020–933	The undivided Kingdom (933 The revolt of Jeroboam)	The earliest Historical Writing
933–721	Israel and Judah (721 Destruction of the Kingdom of Israel)	The First Writing Prophets—Amos, Hosea, Isaiah, Micah
721–587	Judah alone (587 Destruction of Jerusalem)	The Middle Prophets—later Isaiah, Jeremiah, early Ezekiel
587–538	Judah in Captivity (538 Decree of Cyrus permitting the return of the Jews)	Prophets—later Ezekiel, Second Isaiah. Histories—many of the old historical records collected and edited
538–432	The Return to Jerusalem (432 Second visit of Nehemiah to Jerusalem)	Prophets—Haggai, Zechariah, Malachi. History—Nehemiah. Codification of the laws
432–4 BC	The Jews under foreign rule (333 Alexander's conquest of Persia; 168 The Wars of the Maccabees)	Chronicles. The later Psalms Daniel. Many books, such as 1 and 2 Maccabees, found in the Apocrypha

Not all the Old Testament books are indicated in these tables. But constant reference to them will enable the reader at each point to find out where he is in the rather complicated panorama of the Old Testament story.

THE PROPHETS

☐ Israel had had prophets from very early times. But the phenomenon of writing prophets appears only about the middle of the 8th century BC; and the greatest prophecies were written within about two centuries from that beginning; after about another two centuries, this special form of inspiration seems to have disappeared. In many cases, no doubt, these utterances were written down not by the prophets themselves, but by those who had heard and remembered what they said. Part of the difficulty of reading the books of the prophets is that, in almost every case, they are collections of sayings uttered at different times, not always in chronological order, and often without any clear indication of the circumstances to which they refer.

A much deeper difficulty, however, is that the word 'prophet' conveys to the ordinary English reader a meaning very different from that which is found in the Bible, and therefore the readers tend to come to these books looking for the wrong things. The common impression is that the prophet is a man who is constantly seeing visions and foretelling future events. Now it is true that from time to time the Old Testament prophets did see visions, but not very often; and, in most of the cases that are recorded, all that happened was that the prophet was looking at some very ordinary happening, like some men building a wall (Amos 7:7–9), and suddenly saw through the outward object or event to that deep spiritual principle of which it could be taken as an outward sign. And the propets did foretell the future, but only in a much larger context of the knowledge of God; they were so sure of what God is like in the present that they were able to understand his doings in the past, and to see clearly what he would be doing in the future.

No; the prophet is a man who is so overwhelmed by the sense of the nearness and the reality and the holiness of God that he must speak in God's name, sometimes even against his own will, and say 'Thus saith the Lord.' And particularly the holiness of God. Man stands before God who will not let himself be trifled with. God makes demands upon his people for obedience to his holy will. If the people will not obey, then the holiness of God must take the form of judgment and destruction. But God's holiness is also his faithfulness: he does not desire the death of the sinner, and so the prophet can always look beyond the vision of judgment to a vision of a time when God's will will be perfectly obeyed.

The prophets began to write in circumstances which make their message particularly relevant to our own time. The little kingdoms of Israel and Judah were just being drawn out of their isolation, and called to play a part on the stage of history. Palestine has always been a meeting-place of empires. Then it was the border-country between the great empires of Egypt and Assyria (later Babylonia), and so was inevitably drawn into the whirlpool of international politics. This was the time at which a primitive capitalism was breaking up the old simple ordering of peasant society. The rich were getting richer and the poor were getting poorer, and justice was coming to mean no more than the power of the strong to impose his will upon the weak. Religious ceremonies were splendidly observed, but had little effect on the moral life of the people. Men had forgotten that the only way to serve a good God is to be upright, truthful and merciful. God in the international sphere; God in the life of the nation and society; God in his relation to man as a responsible being—these are the great themes of the prophets. Peace, justice, faith—are there any problems that are more pressing and urgent today than these?

It might be thought that the words of men who lived so long ago, and spoke so particularly to the needs of men in little kingdoms that have long since disappeared, would have little to say to us today. It is not necessarily so. The tales of Greece still win and touch the hearts of men. Words such as

> Queens have died young and fair;
> Dust hath closed Helen's eyes

can move us deeply, just because they speak to us of the joys and tragedies of life embodied in the experience of particular men and women. It is just because the prophets spoke so exactly and uncompromisingly to the men of their own day, that they can come to us as freshly as though they had been newly written, and perhaps with a greater and more immediate relevance than the leading article in yesterday's *Times*.

AMOS

Amos is known only from the book that bears his name. He lived and prophesied in the time of Jeroboam II, King of Israel, who reigned from 785 to 741 BC, and had raised his kingdom from a very low estate to a height of considerable prosperity. But Amos came from the southern kingdom of Judah, his home Tekoa being a few miles south of Bethlehem in the Negev.

The four sources of his inspiration are clear from the book: *1.* The handiwork of God in nature, particularly the starry heaven as Amos had seen it, camping out with his flocks; *2.* the stories of the great things that God had done for his people in the past; *3.* the sound of the armies of the nations and perhaps the sight of them marching along the great coastal road; *4.* what his eyes saw and his ears heard in the corrupt and wicked cities of his time. All these sources of inspiration are available to each of us—but only some special pressure from the hand of God makes a man into a prophet.

The central theme of the book is *righteousness*; right dealing between man and man, based on mutual respect, and issuing in a social order which is the expression of justice and mercy. And this can be based only on a right relationship between man and a righteous God.

HOSEA

Hosea was a slightly later contemporary of Amos, but unlike him he was a citizen of the northern kingdom of Israel, and, again unlike him, he seems to have belonged to the settled farmer class. Both prophesied in the same situation—national prosperity allied to national unfaithfulness to God. Much of his book is extremely difficult to understand; it consists not so much of connected discourses as of brief poignant sayings; but there is no doubt of its power and beauty. If Amos is the prophet of the righteousness of God, Hosea is the prophet of the love of God in the Old Testament. His characteristic idea is the loving kindness or tender mercy of God, in which is included the idea of his faithfulness to the covenant that he has made with his people. This is set forth in the strange story of the relations of Hosea with his wife, part of which is given in the one selection from this prophet for which it has been possible to find space in this course of reading.

Amos 3, vv. 1 to 15 (1, v. 1 to 3, v. 15)

The whole of the Old Testament revelation may be said to be summed up in a 'therefore' (compare in the New Testament 'wherefore' in Philippians 2:9). 'I have chosen you' says God '*therefore* I will punish you.' This was the exact opposite of what the hearers of Amos believed, and of what we always incline to believe ourselves: 'I have chosen you; therefore I will help and protect you at all times and in all circumstances regardless of what you do.' They thought that God's covenant was unconditional. It was, in the sense that God is faithful and will not go back on his word. This does not alter the fact that God demands obedience, and that 'to whom much is given of them shall much be required.'

Amos starts his teaching in Samaria, the capital of Israel, by a recital of the sins of neighbouring nations, and no doubt this was for the moment very popular: we all like to hear denunciations of the sins of others. Pleasure must have changed to dismay as he went on to rebuke the oppression and immorality and profanity that obtained in Samaria in his day (2:6–8); and the hearers must have been absolutely horrified when Amos laid down the principle that, because they were God's people, their punishment would be more severe than that which fell upon other nations. But it was so 2,500 years ago, and it is still so today: judgment is to begin at the house of God (1 Peter 4:17).

Prayer *Lord, suffer us not to imagine that privilege can be separated from responsibility, or to suppose that, because thou hast given us the inestimable honour of being called Christians, we shall be in some way exempted from the severity of thy judgments. Help us rather to serve thee in the spirit of humility, righteousness and peace, through Jesus Christ our Lord. Amen.*

Amos 5, vv. 11 to 27 (5, vv. 1 to 27)

The greatest service rendered by the Hebrew prophets was that permanently and for ever they made secure the connection between religion and morality, between believing in God and being good. This has become so much a part of our western tradition that it is hard for us to imagine that it could ever be otherwise; it is well to remind ourselves that both the prophets and the apostles were surrounded by cults in which the wildest sexual indulgence formed a recognised part of worship, and that the same conditions hold in many parts of the world today.

Religion can be regarded as an intellectual concept, a mystical experience, a form of emotional stimulation, a liturgical observance. It can be any or all of these things; but the prophets insist almost monotonously that none of these things is of any value unless it expresses itself in the prosaic, down-to-earth business of being true and honest and kindly in daily life. The Israelites thought that by splendid temple ceremonial it would be possible to keep on the right side of God, and maintained that they were a highly religious people; Amos meets this claim with God's astonishing judgment, 'I hate, I despise your feasts' (v. 21).

There is always a tendency to imagine that there are some areas of man's life upon which God has no claim. In fact in the 19th century a whole philosophy was based on the idea that the laws of economics and religion belong to two different worlds. The prophets will have none of this; God is Lord of all, and everything comes under his judgment. It is because of this clear testimony that even today we find it necessary to turn back to these prophets of old time.

To think over *Today a little self-examination will be in order: how many practices do I allow myself on weekdays (e.g. dodging income-tax) that are not really compatible with what Christians profess on Sunday?*

Amos 7, vv. 10 to 17 (7, vv. 1 to 17)

This dramatic incident leads far into the secret of the nature of prophecy.

Jeroboam I of Israel had established his shrine and sanctuary at Bethel, where Amos is now prophesying. The prophet's purely religious denunciation is at once treated as political disaffection. We see exactly the same distortion in the trial of Jesus. And almost all religious persecutions in Christian history have been given this political colouring.

Furthermore, we see here the inveterate opposition between the priest and the prophet. There is no intrinsic need for this opposition. Yet the priest stands for the ordered, the familiar, the well-established in religion; the prophet challenges all this in the name of new insights and sometimes of demands for revolutionary change.

There is the contrast between the professional and the amateur. There were in Israel 'schools of the prophets', men who seem to have sought an ecstatic inspiration a little like that of the dervishes of North Africa (see 1 Samuel 19:18–24). Nothing could be more unlike this kind of inspiration than the highly poetic, yet sober, reasoned and moral appeal of Amos. He can offer no testimonial, no certificate, nothing but his own intense inner certainty that he has been called by God to prophesy. How this certainty came to him we cannot exactly say; but anyone who has ever tried to follow Christ is familiar with that quiet, persistent, irresistible pressure upon us of some power outside ourselves, which we commonly refer to as the working of the Holy Spirit in our hearts. This is near enough to prophetic inspiration to help us to some understanding of what that inspiration may have been.

To think over   *God never ceases to send prophets to men. Whom would you regard as our contemporary prophets? How far do they resemble the Old Testament prophets; and what have you noticed regarding their reception by the world and by the Church?*

Hosea 2, vv. 1 to 20 (1, v. 1 to 3, v. 5)

In the first three chapters of the prophecy are intertwined the tangled story of the prophet's relations with his wife, and the interpretation of these domestic events as a symbol of God's relationship with his people.

The events are not altogether clear, but the following seems to be a probable outline of them: some time after his marriage, Hosea finds that his wife has been unfaithful to him, and that it is uncertain whether the children born in his house really are his children. He would be entitled to put his wife away and to disown her children. But to his own astonishment he finds that he still loves his wife in spite of her manifold infidelities. At one point, she seems to have fallen so low as to be exposed for sale as a slave in the market; but Hosea buys her back with the produce of his farm (3:1–2).

As he ponders these tragic happenings Hosea feels that it is God who has been guiding him through them all, and at the same time revealing the secret of his own dealings with his unfaithful people. God claimed the exclusive loyalty of his people. But Israel, as it occupied the fertile land of Canaan, found that every valley had its own Baal (lord, husband), the local god of fertility, the giver of corn and wine and oil. The people seem to have imagined that they could combine loyalty to their own great Jehovah, the desert god, with the worship of these local gods, whose rites were often degraded and immoral. Jehovah is depicted as 'a jealous God'; how then is it that Israel has not been destroyed? The answer can only be that, as Hosea still loves his unfaithful wife, so God still loves his unfaithful people; they have not been true to him, but in his unchanging faithfulness he has been true to them. These chapters are a complete answer to those who draw a sharp contrast between 'the angry God' of the Old Testament and 'the loving God' of the New. See also Hosea 11:1–4.

Prayer *Almighty God, whose faithfulness is stronger than our treachery, and whose mercy is greater than our sins, draw us to thyself by the cords of a man, by the bands of love, and make us for ever thy people, through Jesus Christ our Lord.* Amen.

ISAIAH

With Isaiah, we reach one of the greatest heights of Old Testament writing, indeed of human literature. The style of this prophet rolls on in a mighty stream, vivid, concise, intense, with constant plays on words in the Hebrew, which cannot be reproduced in English, the whole informed by a flaming fire of the vision of God, of moral integrity, of penetrating understanding of human character, of passionate exhortation. The character in Victor Hugo's *Les Misérables*, who learned Hebrew simply in order to be able to read Isaiah, had made no bad use of his time.

Amos and Hosea had been concerned with the northern kingdom. Isaiah prophesies in Jerusalem, the capital of the southern kingdom of Judaea. He is closely connected with royal circles, perhaps even himself a member of the royal family, and exercises the influence of a statesman on the policy of his nation. Thus we can date his activity almost exactly in the second half of the 8th century BC. Up to that time, Israel and Judah had been mainly concerned with the small surrounding kingdoms—Syria, Moab and the rest—and Assyria was only a dark cloud on the far horizon; but now the mighty Assyria—hard, remorseless, cruel—one of the first of the world empires, had completed its march to the sea, and was at the doors. The frightened kingdoms turned to political methods and alliances as their only protection against the storm. Isaiah's message is of repentance and absolute confidence in God alone: 'in quietness and confidence shall be your strength' (30:15). At this point, the purpose of God required that Judaea should remain an independent kingdom, and that its sanctuary should remain inviolate; therefore the city would be spared. Contrary to all expectation, God's promise through Isaiah was fulfilled, and Jerusalem was granted another century and a half of life.

Isaiah 36, vv. 1 to 22

Today's reading and that which follows set Isaiah firmly in his place in history. Here is a definite date (v. 1; the date is within a year or two, 702 BC); and a definite event Sennacherib's invasion of Judaea.

In ancient times, wars between peoples were frequently regarded as wars between their gods; and sometimes the victor claimed that he had won his victory because the gods of the defeated people had already passed over to his side. This is the meaning of his claim in v. 10. Was it true? His success had been astonishing; was it really the case that the gods of Assyria were stronger than the God of Israel, or that the God of Israel had already passed over to the side of Sennacherib? This is the anxious situation into which Isaiah has to speak.

The claim of Sennacherib is the human and blasphemous per-version of something that the prophets constantly affirm—that the affairs of all the nations are in the hand of God, and that he can control and use even the pride and ambition of a heathen king for the fulfil-ment of his purposes. The Assyrian is the rod of God's anger (see especially Isaiah 10:5–11); but the last word is with God and not with Sennacherib. Nothing in Old Testament revelation is more vital than this concept of a great purpose of God, which he is working out in and through the whole of human history.

To think over   *We are often told that, on the lines of this prophetic insight, we should see God at work in the great historic movements of our time. How would you apply this (a) to Islam? (b) to Communism?*

Isaiah 37, vv. 21 to 38 (37, vv. 1 to 38)

This episode comes near the end of Isaiah's ministry as a prophet; it has been taken first partly in order to make plain the historical connection of his work, partly because this magnificent poem, in which God's answer to the defiance of Sennacherib is set forth, so perfectly expresses the prophetic understanding of history.

To the outward eye, God is always on the side of the big battalions; injustice is not immediately punished, and the weak are not always delivered. But the prophets take a longer view; the arrogance of men contains the seeds of its own destruction, and kingdoms based on tyranny and rapacity cannot stand for ever. For the time being God may allow them to continue, and may over-rule even their violence for his purposes; but he sets a limit to what they can achieve, and in the end his judgment goes forth in their destruction. To those who lived through the rise and fall of the Hitler regime the words of the prophet may seem to have a poignant relevance.

The most probable explanation of v. 36 is that an outbreak of plague caused a panic in the Assyrian camp, as a result of which the army fled. (Numbers in the Old Testament need never be taken too exactly.) For the moment the danger was past, but it would recur again. Sometimes the prophets seem to paint the future in too rosy colours, as though the immediate crisis were the last, and permanent peace would follow it. Such hopes were often disappointed; yet in the long run the prophetic faith has been justified. Century after century, Israel has been threatened, persecuted, almost destroyed—and yet today we are confronted by the miraculous survival of Israel as a nation. Again and again the Church of Christ has been at the point of destruction; and yet it survives today as the instrument in the hand of God for the carrying out of his will; it has 'taken root downward and borne fruit upward.'

To think over   *'They that be with us are more than they that be with them' (2 Kings 6, v. 16)*

Isaiah 1, vv. 1 to 20

The chapters of Isaiah are not arranged in chronological order, and many of the prophecies it is impossible to assign to an exact date. The first chapter belongs evidently to a date much earlier, perhaps as much as 40 years earlier, than the song contained in yesterday's reading: and it stands as a prologue to the whole book because in it are announced all the themes that will be developed in the symphony of the other prophecies.

Here, as in Amos, is God's detestation of religious ritual unaccompanied by a change of heart (11–15) and his demand for plain common honesty in human dealings (16–17). Here is the idea of the remnant, the small fragment of the nation that is left, and through which, as we shall see later, the purpose of God can go forward, even though the nation as a whole will be destroyed (v. 9). Here is the menacing note of judgment, in which Jerusalem the holy city is compared to Sodom and Gomorrah, the wicked cities of the Plain, which were destroyed (see Genesis 19 and for a remarkable New Testament echo, Revelation 11:8).

Above all, we are shown here the nature of God's approach to his people: 'Come now, and let us *reason* together, saith the Lord' (v. 18). He does not come to terrify them, but to talk things out sensibly, as men do with one another. 'You are not mere animals (v. 3); you have reason and common sense. Look ahead of you, and see what is plain as a pikestaff before you, if only you have eyes to see; and then you will understand.' This is what Job so passionately pleaded for—if only God would meet me as man to man—'Withdraw thine hand far from me; and let not thy terror make me afraid' (Job 13:21). In the prophets this is just what God offers to do; what he begins in Isaiah, he perfects in the Incarnation, where God did in very truth meet us as man to man; and, as in Isaiah, so also in Jesus, the heart of the proclamation is the miraculous offer of the forgiveness of sins.

Prayer *Unwearying God, help us always to be astonished by thy long patience with us thy people; and, when thou drawest near, whether it be in judgment or through the gentle appeal of reason, suffer us not through hardness of heart or dullness of hearing to resist thy call.* Amen.

Isaiah 6, vv. 1 to 8 (6, vv. 1 to 13)

No other passage in the literature of the world depicts as vividly as these eight verses the nature of the encounter between God and man.

The encounter is related to ordinary experience. This is the year that King Uzziah died—738 BC. He had been a great king; he had reigned for 52 years; 'he was marvellously helped till he was strong' (2 Chronicles 26:15)—but he died. There is a felt contrast between the transitoriness of all human power and the unchanging majesty of the Lord of Hosts. The scene of the vision is the earthly temple; the prophet suddenly sees, beyond the visible altar and the smoke ascending from the sacrifices, to the eternal realities which these things dimly shadow forth.

In all such encounters, there are four clearly marked phases:

1. *Conviction* (v. 5). When a man meets God, the first reaction is not exaltation but abasement: 'Who am I that I should stand before a holy God? What am I to do with my sins?' Some men claim to have met God without experiencing this need for penitence, but their claim must be regarded as highly suspect.

2. *Cleansing* (vv. 6–7). The answer is that we do not need to do anything about our sins, since God has undertaken to look after them for us, if we will allow him to do so. The cleansing may be painful, but it is real. How God can bring this about is, of course, fully shown only in the Cross of Christ.

3. *Call* (v. 8). God has work to be done. The mystic may withdraw from other men to enjoy the pleasure of contemplation; the servant of God receives the vision *only* that he may go forth and share it with other people.

4. *Commission* (vv. 9–13). The call is not a general call to service; it is specific and definite for Isaiah, as it will be for us, if we are willing to respond. He is given a task to fulfil that is bound to lead him into unpopularity and suffering; his faithfulness in the fulfilment of his task is the only valid evidence for the reality of his vision.

Praise   *Holy, Holy, Holy, Lord God Almighty,*
All thy works shall praise thy Name, in earth and sky and sea;
Holy, Holy, Holy, Merciful and Mighty,
God in Three Persons, Blessed Trinity.

Isaiah 22, vv. 1 to 14 (22, vv. 1 to 25)

In this exciting reading, we are at the very heart of the Assyrian invasion. To those who are old enough to remember 1939, it is a familiar picture. Home defence has been neglected, and everything has to be done at once; the water supply of the city has to be protected, a clear field of fire has to be provided for the watchers on the walls. Everything is in the confusion of feverish preparation.

Suddenly the picture changes. Hysterical anxiety is changed into hysterical rejoicing. To those who are old enough to remember 1918, this also is familiar. The reaction may have been brought about by some temporary withdrawal of the Assyrians; it may have been a morbid manifestation of despair (v. 13).

But, in either case, God disapproves of the rejoicing of the people just as much as he had previously disapproved of their activity, since neither is rightly based, neither takes account of the reality and the presence of God. A terrible situation must have been reached when God says that he can do no more for a people. And what is this sin that can never be forgiven? Surely it is the sin of *frivolity*, the refusal to take anything seriously, to act with an open-eyed acceptance of the consequences of action. And is this not exactly the besetting sin of the modern world? Religion has become an extra, to be dallied with by those who are interested in that kind of thing; and sin may be entered upon casually, as though consequences could be disregarded, and everything caught up in the moment and the act. Luther has got into a great deal of trouble for once having written in jest 'Pecca fortiter', 'sin boldly'; but personally I would far rather have to deal with the good old-fashioned sinner, who knew what he was about, than with modern man, who appears to live in such a twilight that he is hardly aware that there is a difference between light and darkness.

To think over   *the gods approve*
The depth and not the tumult of the soul.
                                         Wordsworth

Isaiah 33, *vv. 7 to 24 (vv. 1 to 24)*

In a series of short pictures of astonishing rapidity and brilliance, the prophet depicts for us the experiences of the people, still in relation to the Assyrian menace, but reaching out beyond it to fundamental principles of God's activity among men. The main lines are as follows:

1. vv. 7–9. The terrors and the misery of war. The destruction caused by modern war is more extensive than that of old times, but the misery resulting from it is no more intense.

2. vv. 13–16. The reaction of the people to the presence of God in their midst—a repetition on a national scale of that experience which had come to Isaiah in his vision in the temple.

3. vv. 17–20. The miracle of deliverance. The people of the besieged city had actually been able to see from the walls the Assyrian officials measuring and counting their prey (v. 18); and now they have disappeared like grasshoppers in a night.

4. vv. 20–24. The blessedness of the people that have the Lord for their God.

The Assyrian invasion was a brief episode; but the lessons learned by the prophet reach out far beyond that short time. One way of applying these lessons is to *spiritualise* them—that is to interpret them of the inner conflict of the man who is trying to live as a Christian, and of the unfailing resources of God which are available to him. This is valid and helpful up to a point—but only if we remember that the prophet is concerned with the whole of God's dealings with his world —and that his vivid pictures of one time guide our eyes on to a much longer perspective. 'Thine eyes shall see the king in his beauty' (v. 17) will not, in its fullest sense be fulfilled until God has finished all his purposes in time, and is himself 'all in all' (1 Corinthians 15:28).

To think over   *The need will soon be past and gone,*
Exceeding great but quickly o'er ;
Thy love unbought is all Thine own,
*   And lasts for evermore.*

MICAH

Micah is the fourth of the great 8th century prophets, and belongs to exactly the same period as Isaiah, the last quarter of the century. Like Isaiah he prophesied in the southern kingdom of Judah; but whereas Isaiah is the townsman, Micah speaks as the countryman, who has himself felt the bitterness and anguish of oppression. He goes beyond Isaiah, and sees that the wickedness of the city has gone so far that in the end it must be totally destroyed (3:12).

The little book is difficult and confusing, in the main because of the way in which it came to be written down. The oracles were almost certainly not written down at the time they were delivered; they would be remembered and passed on by word of mouth, and in the process would collect around them later material, which had not originated with the prophet himself. Many of the Old Testament books are in this way composite; and there is reason to think that some of the prophecies of deliverance are later than the oracles of doom which they seem to balance and in part to correct.

NAHUM

This little prophecy is one of the parts of the Bible that we can date almost accurately and with certainty. We have already met Assyria as the threatening power in 701 BC. Internal dissension hindered Assyrian expansion for nearly fifty years; but under the great king Assurbanipal (669–c. 630 BC), advance was resumed; the great city of Thebes (No-amon, 3:8–10) in Egypt was sacked in 661 BC, and the whole of western Asia became one world, an Assyrian world. The peoples groaned under the cruel oppressor, but it seemed as though nothing could ever deliver them from such overwhelming power. Then the incredible happened. In 614 BC Assyria was gravely threatened by the Medes and Babylonians; in 612 the great city of Ninevah was captured and destroyed. The prophecy of Nahum is one expression of the almost hysterical joy of the conquered peoples at their deliverance (or at the near prospect of it, if Nahum wrote before 612). Of course, in a sense the people were mistaken; the destruction of one great city did not bring in the golden age, and one oppressor followed upon another. But the fall of any tyrant is an event over which men may legitimately rejoice.

Micah 6, vv. 1 to 8 (vv. 1 to 16)

These verses are in a form of a dialogue between God and his people —the same reasoned discussion as we have found in Isaiah. The prophets always turn back to the great events of history, and particularly to the Exodus, when Israel came out of Egypt. God's love for Israel is not a matter of sentiment, it has been manifested over and over again in action; why then are the people ungrateful? Have they really any complaint to make against their God? (1–5).

The people now answer, asking to be shown how they are to express their gratitude to God. Their questions lie entirely within the sphere of ritual religion and outward observance. The people among whom the Israelites lived *did* sacrifice the eldest son to their god, with the idea that the most precious thing must not be withheld from God (see the story of Abraham and Isaac in Genesis 22:1–19); shall Israel do less for its God than these less enlightened nations? (6–7).

The prophet's answer is one of the high points of Old Testament revelation. He calls religion entirely out of the ritual field on to another and far deeper level—an inner attitude of the spirit expressed in an outward relationship between God and man. But let us not make the mistake of thinking that this is just an ethical standard—as some people delude themselves into thinking that all that is needed is just 'to live by the principles of the Sermon on the Mount'. The third clause is the most important. We become like the God or gods we worship. The God of the Bible is a particular kind of God, whom in these readings we are coming to know; behind all ethical principles lies the question of our relationship to that God, and our willingness to be transformed by him.

To think over   *If Micah 6, v. 8 is the high point of Old Testament revelation at what points do you think that the New Testament revelation in Jesus Christ goes beyond it?*

Nahum 3, vv. 1 to 19 (1, v. 15 to 3, v. 19)

Clearly Nahum is a great poet, with a rich and vivid imagination. But is this a religious poem? Pagan poets have gloried in the destruction of a rival, and attributed the victory to their gods. Is Nahum really doing any more than this?

The answer is Yes. Nahum is pronouncing a moral judgment on the great city, and interpreting its catastrophe as an illustration of the working of the moral law. And history has confirmed his verdict. The Assyrian Empire was based only on force and violence. Its monuments are now only curiosities. We do not owe to the Assyrians any idea in literature, in philosphy or in politics, which is still vital among men (contrast the contemporary Greeks, Hebrews, Indians and Chinese). The pillars of the universe are truth, righteousness, justice and mercy; and no empire can endure which does not rest firmly on these four pillars. (The writer of these notes recalls having preached on this passage on the Sunday after Hitler had marched into Prague in March, 1939.)

Patriotism is a good thing, and it is nowhere condemned in the Bible. But patriotism can be Christian only if it is accompanied by constant and rigid self-criticism. Like others in the past, we think that our civilisation and our order are eternal. But are we sure that this civilisation is so firmly based on righteousness and mercy that we can reasonably expect it to abide for ever?

Prayer *Bless, O Lord, our country . . . and grant unto us not only such outward prosperity as is according to thy will, but above all things, such virtue and true religion that thy holy name may ever be glorified in our midst, through Jesus Christ our Lord. Amen.*

JEREMIAH

Jeremiah, a member of a priestly family of Anathoth, not far from Jerusalem, prophesied during the last forty years of the life of the kingdom of Judah—from about 625 to 586 BC. The first part of this period fell within the reign of the great reforming king Josiah, of whom we shall read in another context; the second in the final period of demoralisation and distress. Jeremiah is one of the most interesting figures of the Old Testament, since he tells us more about his own inner experience than any other. The whole of his ministry was a tragic conflict between his tender love for his people and the hard necessity of proclaiming their inevitable destruction; between his own shrinking timid spirit and the hand of the Lord which drove him out to prophesy, although his ministry made him the object of scorn, hatred and intrigue on the part of his people. He was threatened, scourged, thrown into a horrible dungeon, and in the end was carried away by a fragment of his people to Egypt, where he had no desire to go.

At intervals through his book he carries on a deep and moving dialogue with God. Every mood is revealed, from despair, bitterness and the feeling that God has betrayed him, to a gradually growing submission, trust, and in the end strong confidence and hope. The sufferings and the faithfulness of Jeremiah have made it natural to compare him with Jesus: but his prayer against those who had sought his life—'pull them out like sheep for the slaughter, and prepare them for the day of slaughter' (12:3)—shows how far the Old Testament, even at its highest points, falls short of the revelation of the love of God in Jesus.

Jeremiah 52, vv. 1 to 16 (52, vv. 1 to 30)

A century has passed, and the situation has changed. Ninevah is no more, and its place as a world power has been taken by Babylon, perhaps less cruel than Assyria, but almost equally destructive. The message of Isaiah had been that, in spite of the sin of Judah, Jerusalem would be preserved; a century later his great successor Jeremiah has to give the tidings that the limit has been passed, and that the city will certainly be destroyed.

Between 612, when Ninevah was destroyed, and its own final destruction in 587, the kingdom of Judah lived a feverish life, ruled by puppet kings, torn between submission to Babylon and futile attempts at rebellion with the help of Egypt. And all this time there went on a steady disintegration of the moral fibre of the people—and at last the kingdom came to its irrevocable end. Actually, the number of people deported to Babylon was not very large—the land was not empty; but imagine the effect on the life of a people, when almost all the towns have been destroyed, and all the leaders, all the professional men and all the craftsmen have been carried away. What it felt like can easily be discovered by reading the little book of *Lamentations.*

It seemed as though a final end had come to everything. But God's ends are always new beginnings. New lessons had to be learned in new ways. For a time it had seemed as though God's plan were tied to thè existence of an earthly temple and the survival of an earthly kingdom. Now it was to be shown that the plan could go forward in entire independence of both these things.

To think over *The most difficult verse in the Bible to believe is 'All things work together for good to them that love God' (Rom. 8, v. 28). Have we to any extent in our own experience verified that this is true?*

Jeremiah 5, vv. 1 to 14 (5, vv. 1 to 31)

Josiah has reformed his people's worship; he has not been able to reform their hearts. The opening verse in the chapter inevitably recalls the famous passage in Genesis 18, in which God promises to spare Sodom, if ten righteous people can be found in it. 'Ten?' says Jeremiah; 'Can this wicked city produce a single righteous man?'

The picture is indeed dark. Even the leaders are utterly corrupt. Idolatry (v. 7) is followed by its usual accompaniments of personal immorality (v. 8), and the perversion of justice to the oppression of the poor (v. 28). What makes it worse is that all this is associated with a reckless self-confidence, which refuses to recognise the judgments of God (v. 12); this self-confidence is inflated by the false prophets, who promise the people 'Peace, peace, where there is no peace' (8:11); and by the priests, who assure them that, because the temple of the Lord is there, no evil can happen to the city (7:4). Naturally the people are most unwilling to listen to a prophet who speaks to them of 'righteousness, and temperance, and the judgment to come' (Acts 24:25). If there is no single element left in the people that is sound and true, what can God do in the end but sweep it all away?

To think over *What do you think would be the judgment of Jeremiah if he was prophesying in London or Manchester today?*

Jeremiah 20, vv. 1 to 18

The Bible is full of biographies, but there are very few autobiographies. Many of the Psalms speak to us directly out of the experiences, the joys and sorrows of the writers; but in almost every case the writer is unknown, and we cannot tell from what situation he was writing. St Paul gives us a number of glimpses into his inner life, as does our Lord himself ('My soul is exceeding sorrowful even unto death' Mark 14:34). But Jeremiah is the first to share his confidence with us, and this gives their special value to these parts of his writings. We see that the saints of old were in no way different from us—the fact of divine inspiration did not exempt them from any of the struggles that we pass through; they had to learn to trust God through experience, just as we do; they had to win their victories, as hard won as ours.

This chapter belongs to a late period in Jeremiah's ministry, not long before the fall of Jerusalem. What a variety of emotions is expressed in it! We find complaint (vv. 7–8), anxiety (v. 10), confidence (v. 11), protestation (v. 12), triumph (v. 13); and finally something very like despair. But stronger than anything else is the sense of the inexorable hand of God upon him (v. 9); Jeremiah must constantly have been tempted to give up, to retire into private life; but something has come upon him stronger than himself that will not let him go. The word of the Lord has taken hold upon him. This was the experience of all the prophets; it made Amos say 'The Lord God hath spoken, who can but prophesy?' (Amos 3:8), and Paul cry out 'Woe is unto me if I preach not the Gospel' (1 Corinthians 9:16). Every true Christian will sooner or later have some share of this experience.

To think over   *Does your own experience to any extent confirm that last sentence?*

Jeremiah 31, vv. 23 to 37 (31, vv. 1 to 40)

The greater part of the book of Jeremiah is sad, and heavy with the weight of impending doom. Chapters 31–33 are so different in tone that many scholars have thought that they must be the work of another and later prophet. But there is really no need to suppose this; Jeremiah saw the certainty of immediate judgment on a wicked people, but he did not for that reason imagine that God's purpose in and through Israel had come to an end, and therefore he looked out beyond the days of judgment to better times, when God would restore, and Israel would be worthy of restoration.

The word 'covenant' is immensely important in the Old Testament. It speaks on the one hand of God's choice, and God's faithfulness; on the other of the obligation resting on man to be loyal and obedient. As in this passage (v. 32), the prophets turn again and again to the covenant which God had made with his people when he brought them out of Egypt. Behind that covenant the prophets saw another and older promise which God had given to all men and peoples in Noah after the flood (Genesis 9:8–17; Isaiah 54:9). Jeremiah goes even further back, and sees a covenant of God with the whole created universe, the covenant of day and night (Jeremiah 33:20). But now all these covenants are to be superseded by a new covenant, which will be based on forgiveness, and on an inner and immediate experience and knowledge of God.

Six hundred years later, another Man, another King, with a group of eleven disciples in an Upper Room, told them 'This is my blood of the new covenant, which is shed for many' (Mark 14:24). He was telling them in plain terms that the old promise given to Jeremiah was now fulfilled in him—the New Covenant was here. Every time we come to the Holy Communion, we claim the privileges of that New Covenant. But before we come on to study it, we must do as the prophet so often did—we must look back to the origin, to the making of the people of Israel, to whom the prophets spoke, and to whom in the end Christ came.

To think over 'Old Testament' and 'New Testament' mean simply 'Old and New Covenant'. Do these seem to you suitable titles for the two parts of the Bible?

PROPHECY AND HISTORY

☐ The books which we find first in our Bibles are mostly 'histories'; we must now turn back to take a glance at what is in them. This is a suitable point at which to do this, as these ancient books are books of 'prophetic history'. For the most part they bear no names; we do not know who wrote Judges or 2 Kings, and it is difficult to say exactly when they were written. But it is almost certain that they reached their final form in the period of the end of the kingdom that we have just been considering, or a little later, in the period of the captivity to which we have yet to come. These books contain many elements—old, old tales that had been told endlessly around the camp-fires of the Bedouin, almost contemporary chronicles from the courts of kings, sagas of heroes, fragments of poems and much else. But all these have been brought together, pondered, arranged by the prophetic mind, as it sought to understand the present in the light of the past, and to interpret the actions of God in the history of their own day in the light of God's activity in the long centuries of his education of his people.

Just about the time that these ancient Hebrew history books were taking shape, the Greeks were also beginning to write history. It is most interesting to compare the two types. The Greeks were strong in the understanding of human motive and of political action. What gives its greatness to Hebrew history is its unity in the central idea of a purpose of God in history. Things do not just happen meaninglessly one after the other; they are all related in one way or another to an advancing purpose of God. That purpose has three strands—the land, the people, and the ultimate sovereignty of God over all the earth. We shall not understand the meaning of the histories unless we keep these three aspects constantly in our minds.

Genesis 11, v. 27 to 12, v. 9

History has been punctuated by a great many incursions from 'the Desert' into 'the Sown', and particularly from the deserts of northern Arabia into 'the fertile crescent' running north-westwards from Mesopotamia to Syria, and down through Palestine to Egypt. The stories of the patriarchs are in part the stories of the movements of tribes and clans. But great movements go back to individuals and not to anonymous currents of history, and there is no reason to doubt the historicity of Abraham, though at certain points he comes to us dimly across the mists of nearly forty centuries.

For there is a mystery. We now know a great deal about Ur of the Chaldees, through excavation of the many cities built on that site. It was a heathen city, worshipping many gods. How was it that one man in that atmosphere felt himself constrained to move westwards under the impulsion of a single god, and to find there a promised land? How did the idea grow up that God had a special purpose for that land? How did one primitive Bedouin tribe become convinced that they were in a special sense God's people? *How did it come about that they were right?* Jesus Christ *was* born in the land of Canaan. The people of Abraham *have* made a far greater contribution to the spiritual history of mankind than any other people. Abraham *did* found a spiritual family, into which all the nations of the earth are still being gathered.

Jewish nationalism was often very unlovely in its pride, its exclusiveness, its contempt for others; but it never entirely forgot the promise of its origin. God's plan is always to work from less to more. If he chooses one people, it is in order that through that people his call and his blessing may go out to the very ends of the earth.

To think over *'By faith Abraham, when he was called . . . went out, not knowing whither he went . . . for he looked for the city which hath foundations' (Hebrews 11, vv. 8 to 10).*

'If ye are Christ's, then are ye Abraham's seed, heirs according to promise' (Galatians 3, v. 29).

Genesis 22, vv. 1 to 19

Today's reading is a splendid example of the way in which the Bible takes a very ancient, and even barbarous, story and fills it with spiritual meaning.

'God tempted Abraham'—we are sometimes disturbed by the Hebrew way of attributing everything directly to God, without interposing second causes; but we are quite entitled, if we wish, to translate more in accordance with our own way of speaking 'God allowed Abraham to pass through a period of testing.' And we can easily see how the testing came about. Abraham was surrounded by peoples who had the horrible custom of sacrificing their first-born sons to their god, making them 'pass through the fire to Moloch' (Leviticus 18:21; 2 Kings 21:6). Could God's own men do less for the true God than the heathen did for their false gods? We read in the story of Abraham the anxious questioning of many Israelites over the centuries.

The biblical answer is given in four stages, all of which are implicit in the Genesis story:

1. Human sacrifice is absolutely prohibited.

2. The first-born son was to be regarded as belonging specially to God, and had as it were to be bought back by his family (Exodus 13:2, 13).

3. But this was not to be regarded as meaning that God demanded less from his people than the gods of the heathen—his demand is still for absolute obedience, as is later to be expressed in the command, 'Thou shalt love the Lord thy God with all thine heart, etc.' (Deuteronomy 6:5).

4. It was a true instinct that led the Church to appoint this passage as the first lesson for Good Friday. What right has God to ask such obedience of us? He has the right of One who 'spared not his own Son, but delivered him up for us all' (Romans 8:32).

Prayer *O Lord, who callest thine own sheep by name, grant we entreat thee, that all whom thou callest by the voice of conscience may straightway arise to do thy most compassionate will, or abide patiently to suffer it.*   Amen.

Genesis 28, vv. 10 to 22 (vv. 1 to 22)

Jacob had plotted with his mother Rebekah, deceived his father Isaac, and cheated his elder brother Esau out of the special blessing which was his by right. Now his punishment is to begin—he is to spend twenty years in exile, and never to see his mother again. But the hardest part of the punishment is the thought in his mind that he will be cut off from the worship of his father's God. This idea that God can be worshipped only in his own country is expressed again by David: 'They have driven me out this day that I should not cleave unto the inheritance of the Lord, saying, Go, serve other gods' (1 Samuel 26:19). Jacob finds to his astonishment that it is not so, that God can be with him even in the lands of his exile.

We shall find all through the Old Testament the tension between these two ideas—that the Temple is the only place where God's presence is really to be found (Psalm 63:1–2), and that God is everywhere present (Psalm 139:7–12). It is only in the New Testament that the answer to the question is finally given. Jacob's dream was only a dream; but there was a reality to correspond to that dream. One day the heavens were really to be opened; one day the angels would ascend and descend, not upon a dream ladder but upon the Son of Man (John 1:51), in token that the presence of God would now abide permanently among men, and would be available everywhere to them that seek him in the face of Jesus Christ.

To think over   *Though, like the patriarch,*
                          The sun gone down,
                 Darkness be over me,
                          My rest a stone,
                 Yet in my dreams I'd be
                 Nearer, my God, to thee,
                          Nearer to thee!

Genesis 45, vv. 1 to 16 (45, v. 1 to 46, v. 7)

Next to the biographies of Moses and David, that of Joseph is the
longest in the Old Testament. The whole (Genesis 37–50), which is
one of the most brilliant examples of story-telling in the whole history
of the world, should be read at a sitting.

In the general setting of the Old Testament, this story answers the
important question 'How did it come about that the children of
Abraham, to whom God had promised the land of Canaan, spent
more than 400 years in Egypt?' Joseph, the favourite son of Jacob,
was cruelly betrayed by his brothers and sold into slavery in Egypt.
Years later, when he has become rich and powerful, in time of famine
Joseph invites his father and his brothers to come and settle in
Egypt, and so their long exile begins.

There is more in it that this. The story is set forth in such a way as
to show that those who trust in God are never forsaken, and that his
providence can turn to good ends what appears to be purely evil. At
the same time, we are given the example of most attractive and
generous forgiveness. Joseph will not at once declare his forgiveness; he must first test his brethren, to see whether they are still
actuated by the old cruel and selfish motives. But, when he finds that
time has brought them to a sense of responsibility and compassion,
he offers them his forgiveness, and it is ungrudging and complete.

We do not know exactly at what date the story of Joseph was
written down; certainly it had circulated orally for a long time before
it reached written form, and is of great antiquity. It is surely remarkable that at so early a date we find religious ideas and principles that
are not far short of the New Testament itself.

Prayer *O God, when our hearts burn within us because of the wrongs that others have
done to us, help us to remember the example of thy Son ; and, when it is within our power to
take vengeance, teach us to repay injury with service, harm with healing, and hate with love,
through the same thy blessed Son Jesus Christ.* Amen.

Genesis 50, vv. 1 to 14 (50, vv. 1 to 26)

This last chapter of Genesis speaks of the intense devotion of the people of Israel to their land. Abraham had been a stranger in the land of Canaan, without a single yard of land that he could call his own. So special importance is attached to the first possession that he acquired—a burial-place, where he could bury his wife. In all the story-telling of the Old Testament there is nothing more wonderful than the narrative of the purchase in Genesis 23; it all happens exactly as it would happen today, with the same grave courtesy as is still current among the peoples of the East. There Jacob must return to be buried; and there, in due course, the bones of Joseph must be taken to be laid (vv. 24–25).

Later in our study, we shall read of the yearning of exiles for their land and their city. And today, by one of the strangest reversals of history, forty centuries after Abraham, some three million of them are back there—the State of Israel, an unassimilable phenomenon, a menace to the peace of the world, but to countless Jews the fulfil-ment of a never forgotten dream.

The Old Testament is concerned mainly with three great entities—the Land, the People and the Law. All these were necessary, and exclusive, at that stage of Revelation. The New Testament leads us on to a vision of the time when all the world will be God's Land, all will have become the People of God, and the Law will no longer be something written in a book, but a living word secretly written by the Holy Spirit in the heart of every man. No longer need we care that our bones should be laid in any special place.

To think over *Nation and United Nations—patriotism and internationalism; are these both gifts of God? And if so, how is the relationship between them to be worked out in the light of the purposes of God?*

Exodus 2, v. 23 to 3, v. 15 (2, v. 23 to 3, v. 22)

In the long history of Moses, there are elements of history and elements of poetry. Because of the latter, some have questioned the historical existence of Moses, and the reality of the events in which he is stated to have taken part. But here is the plain fact—at the beginning of the story, the Israelites are an enslaved people in Egypt; at the end, they are just about to enter Canaan with a new sense of being God's people under God's guidance. Such things do not just happen. A movement does not come into existence without a leader; if Moses had not existed, we should have had to invent him to account for the facts!

In the story, Moses is shown with a threefold inheritance—he is an Israelite, a people now oppressed, but still with the glorious memories of Abraham, Isaac and Jacob. Saved from death in time of persecution, he has been brought up to all the wisdom of the Egyptians, with their wonderful civilisation, and has developed a natural aptitude for command. In many years of exile he has shared the free life of the desert, and has learned all the wilderness ways and all the wilderness craft.

But all these things do not make him a leader, until he has met with God 'at the burning bush'. What follows is a classical example of a divine call. There is, first the overwhelming sense of God's presence. Next, a clear vision of a great task to be accomplished. Thirdly, the natural shrinking before a task too great for human resources. Finally, the yielding of man before God, in the assurance that with the help of God the work can be done. Things do not seem to have changed much in thirty centuries.

For further study   *Look back to the story of the call of Isaiah in Isaiah 6, and read the story of the call of Jeremiah in Jeremiah 1, vv. 1 to 19.*

Exodus 14, vv. 10 to 13 (13, v. 17 to 15, v. 21)

It is not possible to fix exactly the date of the Exodus of Israel from Egypt; but it is generally thought to have taken place about the middle of the 13th century BC when, after a period of great strength under outstanding kings, the power of Egypt began to weaken.

Nor is it possible to say exactly what happened in 'the crossing of the Red Sea'. Of course it was not a case of the children of Israel crossing what we now call the Red Sea where it is many miles wide and hundreds of feet deep. A temporary withdrawal of the waters of one of the shallow lakes in the Suez Canal zone is by no means incredible, and we may well suppose something like this to have occurred. What is much more important is that, all through its history, Israel looked back on this as its real beginning as a people. When they were weak and helpless, God did for them what they could not possibly have done for themselves; he brought them out of captivity and set them free; and therefore they were his people. To this the prophets again and again recall the faithless people. And, all through Christian history, the Exodus has been regarded as a type of the far greater deliverance that God has wrought for his people through the death and resurrection of Jesus Christ. St Paul uses the remarkable expression that they 'were all baptised unto Moses in the cloud and in the sea' (1 Corinthians 10:2); and in the Baptism service in the Prayer Book there is an allusion to the crossing of the Red Sea as pre-figuring Baptism. This is a good example of the way in which the New Testament is penetrated through and through by Old Testament ideas, which we are not likely to understand, unless we have first met them in their Old Testament setting.

Prayer *O Lord, who in the death and resurrection of thy Son hast wrought for us a greater deliverance than the Exodus of Israel from Egypt ; grant that we, whom thou hast thus made thy people, may show forth our unending gratitude by living according to thy will, through the same thy Son Jesus Christ.   Amen.*

Exodus 19, vv. 1 to 19 (19, v. 1 to 20, v. 21)

Israel had been brought out of Egypt; that was the negative side of God's dealing with them. We now come to the positive aspect; what had they been brought out of Egypt *for* : The answer is—in order that they might be constituted God's people.

They had come out of the flat familiar Egyptian plain into the terrifying world of bleak uncouth mountains. There are many evidences in this part of the Bible of a period of volcanic disturbances; this mountain was crowned with smoke and flame. In this tremendous setting Moses introduces the people to their God. Clearly it was an overwhelming experience, and one that lived on for centuries in their racial memory. This is a living God, a God of power. In the desert the presence of God is always more vividly felt than in cities or cultivated places, and the Israelites respond to the presence of Jehovah with awe amounting almost to terror. To some extent he always was, in their idea of him, a wilderness God—in the Psalms (18:7-15) and the prophets (Habakkuk 3:3-15) we can still hear his chariots riding across the sky in thunderstorm and fire.

And this was their God. In Egypt they had lived in a land of many gods, and would do so again in Canaan. It was to be a long time before they realised that Jehovah was the *only* God, and they were always being drawn away to the worship of other gods. But they never quite forgot the experience of Sinai—they had a God who had called them, and to whom they belonged.

'Covenant' is not a very good word to describe this relationship in English, since 'covenant' suggests an agreement between equals, and here the initiative is wholly on the side of God. This is a Covenant of *grace*. To be effective, it depends on obedience; but, since God is unchanging, his purpose remains the same, and he will find means to fulfil it. It may be necessary to make a New Covenant in place of the Old; it may be necessary to find a new Israel. But the God of Sinai will not be thwarted, and will find means to carry out his purpose of blessing to all the world.

To think over   *'If we shall deny him, he also will deny us : if we are faithless, he abideth faithful ; for he cannot deny himself!' (2 Timothy 2, vv. 12 and 13).*

Numbers 23, vv. 5 to 24 (22, v. 1 to 24, v. 25)

The Israelites have finished their time of wandering in the wilderness, and are just about to face their second great adventure—the entry into Canaan. This was a time of the movements of peoples, and the migration of Israel is part of the perennial conflict between 'the Desert' and 'the Sown', which continues even in our own day.

The approach of these hardy tribesmen from the desert filled the more settled people with alarm; and, so the story goes, Balak the King of Moab hired Balaam, a non-Israelite prophet, to come and curse them. To the people of that time a blessing and a curse were almost physical things; a father's blessing (Genesis 27) was almost like a physical gift; and a curse, launched by a 'witch-doctor' who had the special power of cursing, was almost like a physical weapon.

In the remarkable story of Balaam, we are not interested so much in that episode of the talking ass, which still causes trouble to literal-minded people, as in the magnificent poems, which have been worked into the story. It is hardly likely that this is what Balaam actually said on this occasion; but these are ancient poems, and give a wonderful picture of the inner consciousness of Israel at a time of simplicity and undiminished vigour.

Note four points in the poems:

1. 'A people that dwell alone'—Israel is unlike any other people, because it has a special vocation, and a special relationship to God.

2. 'The Lord his God is with him' (v. 21b). God actually dwells in the midst of his people.

3. This means that they have a law, and are under an obligation to maintain holiness (v. 21a).

4. As long as the obedience is maintained, Israel is safe under God's protection, and even a curse will be turned to a blessing (vv. 20, 23, RV margin).

Practical work   *Translate the four points in the Balaam poems into modern language, and relate them to the vocation of the Church today.*

Joshua 3, vv. 1 to 17 (3, v. 1 to 4, v. 24)

The next crisis has arrived. Israel, under its new leader Josua, is to enter the land of Canaan. It was a daunting prospect. The people of the land appeared to be far stronger, more civilised, dwellers in cities. In point of fact, theirs was a decaying civilisation, undermined by a corrupt form of worship. Even so, it was a long struggle, and centuries were to pass before the Israelites were fully masters of the land that they believed God had given to them.

But first there was a formidable obstacle—Jordan had to be crossed. We know that even in modern times a canal or river can prove a grave hindrance to an advancing army—and the Israelites were not trained soldiers. It was at this point, as all later Israelite tradition recalled (see Psalm 114) that God intervened a second time, and made their way plain before their face. We can see quite readily the natural explanation of the miracle; a rise of a few feet in the river bed, through volcanic disturbance or for some other reason, would have exactly such consequences as are here described—though this account was written long after, and perhaps the crossing of the river was not quite such an orderly affair as is here depicted.

Most of the 'miracles', or providential occurrences, which the Christian meets with in his experience are of this kind. Two or three quite natural events combine to produce a wholly unexpected consequence, in which the eye of the believer, but the eye of the believer only, sees that God has been at work.

The crossing of the Jordan has left a deep impress, not only on the recollections of the Hebrews, but also on Christian symbolism. Jordan has regularly been taken as a symbol of the narrow stream of death, which we must cross before we can enter our Promised Land. And, as in *Pilgrim's Progress*, the pilgrims know that, even if they will not all get across dryshod, they will all be brought safe to the other side, and so to the city of their desires.

A prayer for pilgrims

> When I tread the verge of Jordan,
> Bid my anxious fears subside ;
> Death of death, and hell's destruction,
> Land me safe on Canaan's side :
> Songs of praises
> I will ever give to thee.

Judges 5, vv. 1 to 31 (4, vv. 1 to 5, v. 31)

The period of the Judges covers the two centuries (or more) between the crossing of the Jordan and the choosing of the first King of Israel, about 1050 BC. Israel was far from having conquered the whole of Palestine. The various clans lived largely isolated and separate from one another, and were exposed to repeated attacks from enemies inside Palestine and from outside it. There was no central authority; it was a time of great disorder, in which there was real danger that Israel's faith in God and its sense of vocation might disappear.

The Judges were local leaders, who arose in times of danger, and wrought heroic deeds. None of them managed to bring the whole of Israel under his control, or to establish a permanent authority. Our two chapters record (first in prose and then in poetry) a local war in the far north of the country, in which the northern tribes were victorious, largely as a result of a violent thunderstorm, which flooded the river Kishon and cut off the Canaanite enemies from their base.

The Song of Deborah is almost certainly contemporary with the events it records, and is thus one of the very oldest parts of the Bible. In vigour of language, vividness of imagination and rapidity of thought it is unsurpassed by any other poem in the Bible. It makes clear that, even in this time of disorder, the separate clans of Israel still felt that they belonged to one another, and that they were the people of God. This was a violent age. But it should be noted that by the standards of the time Jael was fully justified in putting Sisera to death, since for a man to enter a woman's tent in the absence of her husband was the unpardonable crime, which could only be paid for by a life.

To think over   *The Israelites were sure that their cause was God's cause, and that he must be on their side. Are there any circumstances in which a modern nation has the right to feel the same?*

THE KINGDOM

☐ So far, we have seen the Israelites as a loosely organised confeder-ation of clans linked together by a common sense of being the people of God. The time came when it was possible for them to survive only as a more closely organised people under the rule of a single king. The outward precipitating cause was the aggression of the Philistines, a seafaring people who had arrived from the Mediterranean, and settled in south-west Palestine, not long after the arrival of the Israelites by land. The Philistines brought with them the iron age—and, in the warfare between iron and bronze, those who have the iron weapons are always likely to win. The very existence of Israel as a nation was imperilled.

Not all in Israel were agreed about the nature of the kingship, and we can find in the Old Testament traces of the disagreements. Some accepted the monarchy as of divine appointment—it was the will of God that they should have a king. Others regarded the monarchy as the great apostasy—God alone was their king, and the acceptance of an earthly king had brought the people of God down to the level of the other and heathen nations around them.

The idea of theocracy never died out—the earthly king could rule only as the representative of the unseen God. It was perhaps for this reason that the kings of Israel and Judah, unlike the kings of Egypt and other nations round about them, were never regarded as being themselves divine. But they were the anointed of the Lord (Hebrew: *Messiah*; Greek: *Christos*); they played an important part in the worship of the people as well as in its governance; in this sense they were regarded directly as the representatives of God, and, imperfect Christs that they were, they looked forward to and foreshadowed the Coming King, who should reign in righteousness.

---

1 Samuel 9, vv. 1 to 17 (9, v. 1 to 10, v. 16)

This narrative must be extremely ancient; and in its vivid simplicity, even naïveté, takes us back directly to the atmosphere in which Saul was to become king. The young man goes out to seek the lost asses, and finds a kingdom. What was needed at the time was a kind of Viking, a hero who would rally the depressed forces of Israel against the Philistines; and this Saul, with his great physical stature and vigorous martial prowess, was well-fitted to accomplish. In reading this part of the Old Testament, we must put out of our minds all the usual trapping of royalty. Saul has no court, no regular system of administration. He is simply a guerilla chief, who manages to hold around him the nucleus of a standing army, and to build up the beginnings of a national resistance to the national enemy. Nevertheless, the choice of Saul by Samuel was a most momentous step—henceforth Israel is to be a *nation* as well as a people.

There is much in the character of Saul that is highly attractive—courage, generosity, simplicity. But the career of the first king of Israel was to end in tragedy (the Italian poet Alfieri made a famous tragedy out of his story, and Handel's 'Dead March in Saul' is the best known funeral march in the world). A strain of madness early declared itself in his character; this resulted in gloomy suspicion and hatred of David who later overshadowed him, in seeking the spirits of the dead (the eerie story of the witch of Endor, 1 Samuel 28), and in the final overthrow of the battle of Mount Gilboa (1 Samuel 31). But the later glory of David never entirely drove out the memory of the first king, whom David himself commemorated in the words: 'The beauty of Israel is slain upon thy high places: how are the mighty fallen!' (2 Samuel 1:19).

For further study   *Consider, and try to work out, the parallel: Saul, Israel, the Philistines; King Alfred, the English, the Danes.*

1 Samuel 17, vv. 21 to 50 (17, vv. 1 to 54)

Saul, the first king, had proved a failure. Later tradition recognised in David the real founder of the kingdom. As we shall see later, David's character was marred by many imperfections, but he must have possessed outstanding qualities as a leader. He left a kingdom strong and well-organised; he founded a dynasty which lasted for five hundred years: centuries later Jesus of Nazareth was to be known as the Son of David.

Here he first appears on the stage of history as the hero of a saga. The life of a shepherd boy was far from being as idyllic as fancy pictures sometimes represent it. It involved long, exacting days in the wilderness, constantly in danger from wild beasts and wild men. It was a life calculated to produce immense physical strength, courage, resourcefulness and judgment.

David's challenge to the fully armed Philistine was not an act of reckless daring. To hit with a sling-stone the tiny mark presented by that part of the enemy's head which was unprotected by his helmet demanded extraordinary skill and precision, and in the circumstances an iron nerve. And the first shot must be successful; otherwise David would have no protection against Goliath's spear. David must have known that long practice in the desert had given him the necessary skill.

But, here as everywhere in the Old Testament, the emphasis rests upon the spiritual significance of the situation. Like other battles, this was regarded as a battle between the gods of the respective nations. David was convinced that he was standing as the champion of the cause of the true God, and that victory, if it came, would come not only through his own skill, but because God was with him. Was he wrong in thinking this?

To think over   *Some modern readers have felt that it was 'unsporting' on David's part to attack with long range weapons an adversary who had none. Does this objection seem to you well-grounded?*

2 Samuel 12, vv. 1 to 25 (11, v. 1 to 12, v. 25)

If possible the whole story from 11:1 to 18:33 should be read. This brilliant narrative, which must be nearly contemporary with the events that it records (*c.* 980 BC), is reckoned by many experts to be the earliest piece of connected historical writing in the world; and as such, apart from its deep moral significance, is well deserving of attention.

One of the great qualities of the Bible is that it conceals nothing; it tells of the failures of its heroes (David, Peter), no less than of the crimes of its villains (Judas Iscariot). David was a great hero; but he behaved disgracefully. He lusted after a woman; he cleverly arranged for her husband to be killed, apparently by accident, in battle; and then took her to be his wife. And then apparently everything went on as before.

But Israel was not as other nations; there even the king was subject to the law of God; the law of God had been shamefully violated, and even the king must be rebuked. Nathan must have known that, in going to beard the old lion in his den, he was taking his life in his hands. The remarkable thing is that, when faced with the terribleness of his guilt, the king is willing to accept the rebuke and to repent.

Sin can be forgiven, but its consequences cannot always be trammelled up. Disaster falls on David's family and the kingdom, and for much of this David himself is reponsible. God will not shield us from the consequences of our sins; but, if we sincerely repent, he will stand by to see us through.

To think over   *'Thou art the man.' What are the favourite excuses, by which we try to blind ourselves to the knowledge of our own wrongdoing? Do we too need a Nathan to tell us the truth?*

1 Kings 10, vv. 1 to 13 (10, vv. 1 to 29)

Several of the great trade routes of the world run through Palestine
and Syria. A king of Israel who was strong enough to control these
trade routes and to exact toll and customs from the merchants passing along them could hardly fail to become rich: if at the same time
he himself engaged prudently in trade, he would be likely to become
very rich indeed. This is what seems to have happened in the time
of Solomon. The visit of the Queen of Sheba (in Arabia Felix) was
almost certainly a trade mission as well as a diplomatic courtesy. But,
as presented to us in 1 Kings, this is a profoundly religious narrative;
Solomon is seen as God's own appointed king, sitting safely upon
his throne because the favour of God is upon him.

To one strain of Israelite thinking the age of Solomon presented
itself as the ideal age. Solomon is shewn as a paragon of wisdom—
he could decide rightly in the hardest cases; as a nonpareil of piety—
he built the temple; and as unequalled in glory—silver was nothing
accounted of in Jerusalem in his days. But there was another side
to the picture. Solomon's wisdom did not guard him against failure
to notice the growing resentment of his people at the increasing
burdens of taxation and service that were laid upon them. His piety
did not prevent his corrupting the religion of Israel by building in
Jerusalem shrines for the gods worshipped by his foreign wives. His
glory could not endure, because, like that of Spain when the gold and
silver of the Indies were pouring into her, it was not based on solid
economic foundations. When Christ came, he was to be known as the
Son of David, but never as the Son of Solomon.

To think over *'I say unto you, that even Solomon in all his glory was not arrayed like one
of these' (Matthew 6, v. 29). In the light of this saying, what judgment do you think Jesus
would have passed on the kingdom of Solomon?*

1 Kings 18, vv. 20 to 46 (17, v. 1 to 18, v. 46)

Elijah belongs to a date about a century earlier than Amos and Hosea; although he is a much more violent and tempestuous figure than they, we can see that like them he acts under an irresistible impulse to speak the Word of the Lord, and that, like Nathan, he is mostly deeply concerned with the moral implications of being the People of God.

King Ahab had married Jezebel, the daughter of the King of Tyre. Tyre was a great trading city, the mother-city of Carthage. The Tyrian Baal, whose worship Jezebel wished to introduce in Israel, was quite different from the local Baals of the valleys, whose simple worship the Israelites thought that they could combine with that of their own God. This was an organised religious system; and, if Jezebel had been successful, the worship of Jehovah would have been brought to an end. It was necessary for the people to make a decisive choice—Baal or Jehovah; this is the Old Testament form of our Lord's challenge, 'No man can serve two masters'.

The scene is extraordinarily dramatic with its contrast between the dervish-like prancings of the priests of Baal, and the humble prayer of Elijah, who has waited, tense but patient, all day for the moment of the manifestion of God's power—the lightning-flash that marks the end of the long period of drought. What we see here is the essential contrast between magic and religion. Magic represents man's desire to control the unseen powers for his own advantage, and his belief that he can so control them. Religion is man's humble submission to the unseen powers, his willingness to do God's will. Between these two there is an absolute contrast, and no reconciliation between them is possible.

For self-examination *How much magic, and how much religion, is there really in our ideas about God, and in our attitude towards him?*

1 Kings 21, vv. 1 to 24(vv. 1 to 29)

Even in the Old Testament there is no story more brilliantly told than this. Not a single word is wasted; every character stands out—the king almost childish in his disappointment, the queen masterful and ruthless, the craven elders of the village, the prophet confident in the righteousness of God—as in a first-class etching. Many such acts of unscrupulous injustice have taken place in human history: not every one has found such an author to immortalise it.

Naboth was quite right. In Israel a man had only a life-interest in he land, which was regarded as belonging to the whole family; and no man had a right permanently to alienate any part of it. In order to carry out their purpose, Ahab and Jezebel managed to break a record number of the commandments. Ahab coveted the field (10). Jezebel arranged for false witness to be borne against Naboth (9). On the basis of false charges of blasphemy and treason Naboth is judicially murdered (6); and, since the property of anyone so executed passed to the crown, the vineyard was conveniently appropriated (8).

Everything seemed to have gone according to plan. But they had forgotten Elijah, and that meant that they had forgotten God. Naboth was dead; the land had been taken and there was nothing that Elijah could do to put right the injustice. He could and did point to a larger perspective. The world really is made in a particular way. Its pillars are justice and mercy. You may go against these, and seem to get away with it for a long time; the life of the individual may be too short for the results to be seen; but in the larger life of the nation it becomes apparent that justice is the way of life, and injustice is the way of death. We can forget about God for a very long time; but in the end it really does not pay.

Prayer   *O thou who ordainest the powers that be*
             Grant to our great men, to do nothing against the truth, but all things for the truth,
             To the courts of law, thy judgments and righteousness, to judge in all things
             concerning all without preference and without partiality, through Christ our Lord.
             Amen.

2 Kings 5, vv. 1 to 19 (5, vv. 1 to 27)

Elisha (towards the end of the 9th century BC), the successor of
Elijah, is a much less dominating and volcanic figure than his master.
He is more of a pastoral prophet, and in the stories about him gracious
and kindly features prevail.

In the story of Naaman, the central point is not the miracle of
healing, but the question whether a Gentile could be saved or not.
We shall find at all times two conflicting strains in the Jewish tradition. On the one hand there is the vivid sense of being God's people;
the good side of this was the sense of responsibility for avoiding
contamination by the gods and the deeds of the heathen; the bad side
of it was a harsh and unlovely narrowness and contempt for other
peoples. On the other hand, there is the understanding, which we
have already found in the story of the call of Abraham (Genesis 12:1–9)
that Israel is called in order that a blessing may come to all peoples.
This was never fully grasped until the coming of the Holy Spirit at
Pentecost; but from time to time the great idea dawned that even
Gentiles could become by faith partakers of the privileges of the
people of God. The Old Testament soldier Naaman was a forerunner
of that other Gentile soldier, of whom our Lord was to say 'I have not
found so great a faith, no, not in Israel' (St Matthew 8:10).

Here, as in other stories, we shall notice the precise delineation of
character; but it is easy to overlook the fact that the most important
character of all is the 'little maid'. If she had kept her information to
herself, the story of Naaman would never have been written. We
never know what we may be starting by what we say and do.

To think over   *The three greatest churches of the ancient world were Antioch, Rome and
Alexandria. We do not know the name of any of the founders of any of these churches. Has
this a message for us who are not very wise or mighty or powerful?*

2 Kings 23, vv. 1 to 15 (22, v. 1 to 23, v. 25)

Our history now jumps on nearly two centuries to the time of Jeremiah. Today's reading is the record of the great reformation put in hand by the young king Josiah (640–609 BC). Various attempts had been made before to purify the religion of the Jews from alien and corrupting elements; but this was far more thorough than any that had gone before.

The reform is associated with the discovery of a book in the house of the Lord (22:8). This book is generally taken to have been the book Deuteronomy, 'the book of the love of God in the Old Testament', in which the deep spiritual principles of the old laws are most fully worked out. On the basis of this code the king set himself to work on a thorough renewal of the religious life of his people; his aims were to expel every corruption that had come in through the influence of the surrounding pagan nations; to centralise the worship of the people in the Temple at Jerusalem; and to extend these principles to the territory of the northern kingdom of Israel, which had lost its independence to Assyria more than a century before.

For the moment the reform was successful. There can be no doubt of the sincerity of the king. He was helped by the most spiritually-minded of his people; among whom, of course, Jeremiah was one. But in the end the result was disappointing; once the strong hand of Josiah was removed, or even earlier, things went back very much to what they had been before, For this three reasons may be suggested:

1. A reform directed purely from above is unlikely to have deep and lasting effects.

2. Life and worship affect one another very intimately; but to regulate the worship of a people does not mean necessarily to change their basic ideas about God.

3. The book of Jeremiah shows that the majority of the people were not ready to face the deeper challenge to change their whole way of life. There were lessons, as we shall see, that they could learn only by the way of humiliation and suffering.

To think over *Is a parallel to be observed between the experience of the Jews under Josiah, and the English under King Henry VIII?*

Deuteronomy 6, vv. 1 to 15 (6, vv. 1 to 25)

In opening Deuteronomy, we shall at once be conscious of the change of style from everything that we have previously read. Here we have no longer the sharp, picturesque sayings of the prophets or the vivid rapidity of Hebrew history: this is the flowing rhetorical style of the earnest preacher. He comes back again and again to the same points, and leaves us in no doubt as to the lessons that he wants us to learn. Bacon's saying 'Prosperity is the blessing of the Old Testament, and adversity of the New' is rather applicable to this book; there are deep spiritual truths not to be found in it. But it is a beautiful book, and one which our Lord had deeply pondered, as is evident from the fact that all his answers in the story of the Temptation are drawn from it, and that he took over and made his own the great commandment, as we have it in today's reading.

The main emphases of the book are:

1. God's gracious choice of Israel, depending only on his love, and not on any merit or excellence in Israel.

2. God's gracious care of Israel in all its history.

3. God's gracious demand that his love should be met by an answering love on Israel's part.

4. The judgment that must follow if this gracious invitation is refused.

Is there any other religion on earth that bids its worshippers love their God? Others are invited to fear their gods, to bargain with them, to cajole them, to submit to them. But love? How has the idea got about that the God of the Old Testament is nothing but a jealous tyrant? Is it possible that this idea has been spread by those who have never read the Old Testament for themselves?

Prayer *Pour into our hearts such love toward thee, that we, loving thee above all things, may obtain thy promises, which exceed all that we can desire; through Jesus Christ our Lord.* Amen.

Deuteronomy 24, vv. 10 to 22

The central part of the book of Deuteronomy restates the laws of Israel, using some very old material, and adding a good deal that is new. Comparison with older parts of the Bible shows various ways in which the law had been made gentler as time went on; even the bird on its nest is not forgotten (22:6–7), and there is constant emphasis on the right of the widow, the fatherless and the stranger.

In today's passage, the most striking verse is v. 16. In earlier times a man's family had been regarded as a part of himself, and, if the head of a household was condemned to death, it was customary for his whole family to perish with him. Such a sentence had been carried out in the case of Achan, the first man to commit a sin after Israel had entered the promised land (Joshua 7:24–26). It is interesting that we find in 2 Kings 14:6 a case in which this old barbarous custom was *not* followed. We can see in this development the growth of a gradually increasing sense of the importance of the individual, a process which we shall note again in later books of the Old Testament. But what underlies the change is far more a deeper and better understanding of what God is really like.

If we have once grasped the principle of God's patient and gradual self-revelation to his people, we shall no longer be troubled by anything archaic or barbarous that we find in the Old Testament. Of course it had to be that way. It is of intense interest to follow the progress of understanding, of which today's reading gives us a specimen. The Old Testament at its highest, as in yesterday's reading, can never be out of date. But for us Jesus Christ is always the touchstone, and the truth. The Old Testament points to him, and prepares the way for his coming; but, when he goes beyond the Old Testament revelation, it is to Jesus Christ that we hold fast.

For meditation *'God, having of old time spoken unto the fathers in the prophets by divers portions and in divers manners, hath at the end of these days spoken unto us in his Son.'* (Hebrews 1, vv. 1 and 2)

CAPTIVITY AND RETURN

☐ We have now for the second time followed the experiences and fortunes of the Jews down to the great turning point of the destruction of Jerusalem and the end of the Kingdom of Judah. Between 610 and 587 BC Jerusalem was several times besieged and captured by the Babylonians; and each time a number of captives were carried away to that distant land. The actual number of those carried away was not very large; but, when almost all its leaders and all its craftsmen have been removed, a simple society very soon sinks into a state of squalid barbarism; and this is what seems to have happened to those who were left behind in Palestine.

So for two generations the life of the people went on in two parallel but separate streams. The Palestine Jews claimed that they were the true seed, because they had the land and at least the site of the temple, if no longer the temple itself. But in truth it was among the Exiles that the important things happened. This was very surprising to them; their religion had been so tied up with the holy land and the holy place that it had seemed to them hardly possible that they would be able even to worship God in an unclean land. Yet it was there in the land of exile that they were brought through some of the deepest spiritual experiences of all that are recorded in the Old Testament. There were three lines along which they were led into new truths:

1. A far deeper sense of sin. They rethought the whole of the history of their nation, and saw it, from Egypt to Babylon, as the record of the wonderful patience of God with a people that at every point had spurned his kindness, rebelled against him, and flung itself into evil ways.

2. A less nationally conditioned idea. They lived surrounded by the gigantic idols of the world empires, as we can see them today in the British Museum. What had they, the people of a defeated tribal God, to oppose to such overwhelming might? The answer came in the form of a deeper faith in God as the Creator of the ends of the earth. Once this truth had been firmly grasped, and expressed again and again in prophecy and poetry, never again were the Jews in danger of falling into idolatry.

3. The truth of forgiveness. The people had deserved to be destroyed. They had been very nearly destroyed—but not quite. They still lived, and lived as a people. How could this be? The only possible answer was that God had not cast off his people, that he had forgiven their sin, and that what had appeared to be the end of all things was really the beginning of a new stage of his purposes. So, when a great prophet arose and held out to them the hope of return to their own land, some of them were prepared to listen; and in due course the Exile was followed by the Return.

EZEKIEL

The book of Ezekiel is long and difficult, and raises many intricate problems of interest only to technical scholars; but those who are willing to dig in it will find some of the richest treasures in Old Testament revelation.

Ezekiel was born in Palestine somewhere towards the end of the 7th century BC, and was carried away to Babylonia in one of the first groups of captives. His first vision came to him in the year 593, and after that he seems to have prophesied for a time in Jerusalem, returning to the East sometime before the final destruction of the city. This explains the sharp contrast between two different aspects of his preaching—before the destruction of the city, violent denunciation of the wickedness of the people; after it, that tender pastoral care, devoted to building up the confidence of the exiles, which makes him one of the great prophets of hope.

Ezekiel was probably a priest, and was intensely concerned about holiness, both moral and ritual. His visions end with a picture of a restored and glorified Jerusalem, which had a tremendous influence both on later Judaism and on some New Testament thinking.

Psalm 137, vv. 1 to 9

Today, when there are so many millions of refugees in the world, it is easy for us to understand how terrible a thing exile can be. To be torn up from all your roots, to be homeless, and purposeless and hopeless—what life is that for a man? But for the Jews the most terrible thing of all was the feeling that they had left God behind. 'How shall we sing Jehovah's song in a strange land?' does not mean 'How can we sing, when we are so sad'; it does mean 'The only place where Jehovah's song can be sung is in Jehovah's sanctuary: that sanctuary is far away, and in any case it has been burned with fire'. As we have already said, God showed these exiles better things than this, but at least at the start of the Exile that is what it felt like.

All through the centuries Jerusalem has had this magical fascination for the Jews. Passover has been celebrated year after year with the thought, 'Here this year, perhaps next year in Jerusalem.' And for Christians too; witness the Crusades, and the strange fact that for nearly a century a Christian king reigned in Jerusalem. The second destruction of Jerusalem in AD 70 was almost as much a blow to the infant Christian Church as it was to the Jews. So hard is it for us to learn that 'we have not here an abiding city, but we seek after the city which is to come (Hebrews 13:14).

We should be happier with this Psalm if the last three verses were not there. Various attempts have been made to soften them down or to explain them away; but we are now sufficiently at home with the Old Testament to know better than this. Without the grace of Christ this is what men are like. Those who are old enough to remember the kind of things the Germans said about us and we said about the Germans in the first world war will realise that men are still the same —and it is only the grace of Christ that can turn them into anything different.

To think over   *Is the plight of the refugees today a burden on your heart? What, if anything, have you done to alleviate their lot?*

Ezekiel 33, vv. 1 to 20 (33, vv. 1 to 33)

'Our sins are upon us, and we pine away in them.' This was the natural reaction of the exiles. Sin was thought of almost as a physical substance, a literal infection which a man could not get rid of, and which made him repulsive to God. Ezekiel meets this despairing cry in three ways.

1. First, he gives a great assurance as to the nature of God: 'I have no pleasure in the death of the wicked.' God judges sin and punishes it, but he does not hate the sinner; his one purpose is to bring his people back to himself.

2. For those who have sinned repentance is possible; and the penitent man will be accepted by God. The word 'forgiveness' is not used, but the idea is not far away; though there is more emphasis on 'doing that which is lawful and right' (v. 14) than on inner attitudes of mind and spirit.

3. This makes possible a direct appeal to the individual. The people as a whole may have sinned; it may be that the people as a whole will not repent. But this in no way prevents the individual from turning back, and, as it were, making his own covenant with God. This goes rather further even than the doctrine of 'the Remnant'. Revelation is moving away from the nation to the individual, and we begin to see the possibility of a spiritual Israel, which is not limited by birth or national origin.

Today's reading carries us a long way, but not all the way. It does not answer the deepest question of all: 'I could repent, if I wanted to, but I don't want to. How do I learn to want to?' We are still a long way from the Cross of Christ.

For further study   *If you have a Prayer Book, look up the last two prayers in the Commination Service, and note the echoes of Ezekiel. How much of these two prayers can you make your own?*

Ezekiel 37, vv. 1 to 14 (37, vv. 1 to 28)

In the whole of the Old Testament there is no more vivid or stirring vision than this; and we can well understand what encouragement it must have brought to the despairing Jews. Some forms of later Judaism certainly believed in a physical resuscitation of all faithful Jews, in order that they might have a share in a Kingdom of God to be established upon earth. It may be that the prophet's own horizon was limited to such ideas. But clearly the vision is capable of much wider application:

1. In the history of the Jews: again and again they have seemed to be on the point of extermination, the last great attempt being Hitler's massacre of six million Jews. But it has not happened, and today the Jews are a greater influence, and perhaps a greater danger, in the life of the world than ever before.

2. In the life of the Church: again and again it has seemed to become so dead and corrupt that renewal has appeared impossible; yet God has brought it about and the dead bones have come to life—in the 13th century through St Francis, in the 16th century through the Reformation, in the 18th through John Wesley; and some signs of stirring in our own day.

3. In the individual: anyone who has been truly converted and found new life in Christ, reading these verses, will say, 'Here is my own history!'

Prayer *Lord, increase our faith ; and, if we are confronted by the dry bones of materialism in the world, sloth and self-complacency in the Church, and deadness in ourselves, help us to believe that it is not beyond thy power to command life out of death, healing out of sickness, and glory out of shame, through him who died and rose again, Jesus Christ our Lord.* Amen.

THE SECOND ISAIAH

When Ezekiel had ceased speaking, there was silence for about a generation. Then a great unknown prophet took up again the word of hope. It is almost universally agreed that, though Isaiah chapters 40–66 came in time to be bound up with the prophecies of the 8th century Isaiah, in reality they belong to the period, two centuries later, when the exile of Judah was nearing its end.

Here we come to the climax of Old Testament revelation. It may almost be said that, if the whole of the rest of the Old Testament had been lost and Isaiah 40–55 had been preserved, we should have almost all that is essential in the Old Testament message. In simple, majestic poetry, the prophet develops a few great themes: God, the Creator, is Lord of all the nations as well as of Israel; it is his own honour that is at stake, and this must be vindicated by the deliverance of his people; it is not without God's direction that the new conqueror Cyrus has arisen, and he will set the people free; but free, not for its own sake, but for a wider purpose—'I will also give thee for a light to the Gentiles, that thou mayest be my salvation unto the end of the earth' (49:6).

Here we touch the New Testament and the *Nunc Dimittis.*

Isaiah 40, vv. 1 to 17 (40, vv. 1 to 31)

Another great crisis in world history is at hand. Babylon like Nineveh had seemed impregnable, but now Babylon too is destined to fall before a conqueror. In historic fact, Cyrus conquered Babylon in 538 BC, and established the Persian Empire. As before, a great prophet stands by, watches the processes of history, and interprets them in the light of the divine purpose.

But nothing could be more unlike the ordinary political commentator than our prophet. He foresees the deliverance of his people. But in every chapter and at every point God is in the centre of the stage, this is a message about God and from God.

This is a message about a God who *acts.* He is not an idea, or a unifying principle, or a world-soul. He is a God who comes into history—'the Lord God will come as a mighty one' (v. 10), and when he comes great things happen. Three aspects of God's character are stressed in this book:

1. *Power* (vv. 15–17). Who would think of comparing the gods of Babylon, Bel and Marduk and the rest of them, with this one great God, who made and rules all things? He is not the God of the Jews only but also of the Gentiles (Romans 3:29).

2. *Wisdom* (vv. 13–14). To the mere human observer, history looks like chaos; it is hard to find any principle that holds it together and makes sense of it—so much so that many modern historians have abandoned the attempt to find any such principle. But the prophet's eye can penetrate beneath the surface, and see all that happens as part of a great and manifold purpose of God, a purpose which in its broad outlines we understand.

3. *Tenderness* (v. 11). 'He shall feed his flock like a shepherd.' It's hardly necessary to comment on these words, since even the un-musical reader is likely to be familiar with the most beautiful air that Handel ever composed. In the *Messiah* as a whole, Handel has marvellously caught the spirit of this prophecy.

To think over *Is there such a thing as a Christian interpretation of history? If we maintain that there is, how can we meet the objection that we are simply reading our own ideas into history, and finding something in it that is not really there?*

Isaiah 44, vv. 1 to 17 (44, vv. 1 to 28)

Man is always inclined to make images of the gods he worships, and true religion has always had to battle hard with this tendency to idolatry. Those who live in a non-idolatrous country may be inclined to say, 'Does it very much matter?' The answer is that it does, for four reasons:

1. No image can ever bear any resemblance to the transcendent majesty of God.

2. Historically idolatry always has been, and still is, associated with cruelty and lust.

3. An idol is not just a statue; in most idolatrous countries a ceremony is performed through which the spirit of the god is believed to come and live in the image.

4. The impression is inevitably given that God is *more* in one place than in another. Even Old Testament religion easily fell into this error.

Today idolatry finds defenders, who say to Christians, 'After all, you make images of your God in your minds; what is the difference?' Now, apart from the fact that a mental image is very different from an image of wood or stone, there are three other points to be made:

1. The Christian does make mental images of God or of Christ; but he recognises this as a weakness, from which he would gladly be free.

2. The Christian is not tied to one set of images—those which he makes change with his growth in spiritual perception.

3. In prayer at its highest, the Christian makes no mental image, but is simply conscious of a presence of God which fills his whole being.

For all that, the kind of pictorial representation of Christ which has been current in the Churches has been positively harmful to the understanding of Christian truth. It might have been a good thing if every representation of Christ had been forbidden from the beginning.

To think over *Are missionaries to simple people right to forbid from the start all use of images by Christians? Is there a possible transition stage between idolatry and the purely spiritual worship of Christianity?*

Isaiah 52, v. 13 to 53, v. 12

One of the most noteworthy features in this great prophecy are four 'Servant Songs'—42:1–9; 49:1–6; 50:4–9; 52:13—53:12. Who is this servant? Scholars have exercised their wits on this problem, and propounded every possible kind of solution. At times the servant seems to be Israel; at others, the 'Remnant', the small group of the faithful in Israel; at others the Songs seem to point to an individual, at times as though the prophet were writing out of his own experience of failure and rejection. It may be that these solutions are not really mutually exclusive—there is perspective beyond perspective; and we can see that the prophecy could not really be understood until One came in whom all the purposes of God through Israel were fulfilled.

It is almost certain that Jesus had deeply pondered these passages, and had found in them the explanation of his own vocation. There are only the faintest traces in earlier Judaism of the idea of a suffering Messiah; Jesus brought together the Messiah who was to deliver his people, and the Servant who was to suffer for their sins; and there stood Jesus! It is even more certain that the early Christians used this passage to help them in their understanding of what Jesus had done. Countless times, like Philip, 'beginning with this scripture' they preached Jesus (Acts 8:35).

'By his stripes we are healed.' How? In this life we have to suffer for and because of one another. Those who have not lived through it can hardly imagine the suffering of a young man who has to live knowing that his father is in jail for embezzlement, and that everyone knows it. Suffering is an evil thing; Jesus showed that, when the innocent suffer gladly, suffering itself can be turned into the instrument of redemption.

Here is what Pascal called the greatness and the misery of man. 'All we like sheep have gone astray.' There is the misery of our condition. 'The Lord hath laid on him the iniquity of us all.' There is our greatness; but we are great only because of the greatness of God's redemption.

To think over   See, from his head, his hands, his feet,
                 Sorrow and love flow mingling down ;
              Did e'er such love and sorrow meet,
                 Or thorns compose so rich a crown ?

THE END OF THE OLD TESTAMENT

☐ It cannot be pretended that the end of the Old Testament is as interesting as some of the earlier parts. It is the story of a broken and afflicted people, desperately trying to hold on to the faith of their fathers, and to keep alight the flame of faith in God.

In 538, Cyrus, the new monarch of Persia, gave permission for those of the Jews who wished to return to their own country. Many had settled down and become prosperous in Babylonia, and had no wish to move. But during the next century a number of parties braved the dangers of the desert journey and went back to the house of their fathers. Life was very difficult for them. Those who had remained in Palestine had become disorganised and demoralised, and were not too ready to welcome those who returned. The half-Jewish, half-heathen inhabitants of the old northern kingdom, starting as uncertain friends, became implacable enemies—the Samaritans with whom the Jews have no dealings (John 4:9). False complaints against the Jews went back to the Persian kings. Across the Jordan, the Edomites were anxious to prevent Judaea from becoming again a kingdom and a threat to their independence.

The first great event in this period was the rebuilding of the Temple —a poor thing compared with the glory of Solomon's temple; yet as Haggai foresaw, the glory of this latter house was to be greater than that of the former (Haggai 2:9), not, as he expected, through the streaming in of all the wealth of the Gentiles to it, but because it was to this temple, enlarged and beautified by Herod, that in due time Jesus came. Haggai and Zechariah are true prophets; but it is only occasionally they rise to the great inspiration of the earlier prophets.

The great event of Ezra's time was the final codification of the Law of Israel, and its imposition upon all the people. But it is difficult to date the work of Ezra, and to know exactly when this took place. By contrast, in the Book of Nehemiah, we have something unique in the Old Testament—large extracts from the memoirs of one of the actors on the stage of history. Nehemiah's two visits to Jerusalem can be dated exactly in 444 and 432 BC—the age of Pericles in Athens. His book is of intense interest, not only because of the events that it records, but also because it reveals the character of a simple, high-minded and devoted man.

In 333 BC, the Persian Empire was overthrown by Alexander the Great, and Palestine passed under the power of the Greeks. The most memorable event of this period was the attempt of Antiochus Epiphanes in 168 BC to impose Greek ways and Greek worship on the Jews; the result was one of the first great religious persecutions recorded in history. This is narrated in the books of the Maccabees in the Apocrypha. But it has also left its mark on the Old Testament, since the Book of Daniel in its present form (though it contains older material) most probably belongs to this period. In a series of superb stories, known to every Sunday School child, the writer tries to hearten his suffering people by the assurance that even in time of persecution God has not forsaken them. Towards the end of the book, he gives us the first specimen of what the scholars call 'Apocalyptic'. The prophets had spoken directly to their own times: the Apocalyptist looks on to the end of the world, and foresees the vast calamities through which the Kingdom of God will at last be brought in. Our last reading in this section is from this book; and, as will be seen, this makes a real link with the New Testament, since this passage had a profound influence on the thought of our Lord and his Apostles.

Ezra 3, vv. 1 to 13 (3, v. 1 to 4, v. 6)

It is very significant that the rebuilding of Jerusalem starts with the setting up of the altar, and the laying of the foundation of the temple. No doubt it was a poor enough affair—the people were few and weak, and had not the great resources of the time of Solomon. But their effort indicated what they now were. Israel had been a people, bound together by the ties of kinship. They had been a kingdom, made one by loyalty to the king who was God's anointed. Henceforward they are to be a religion—that is the one central point at which they can be held together. And that in fact has been what has held them together over more than twenty centuries since the days of Jeshua and Zerubbabel; a patient, at times fanatical, adherence to the Law of their God and to the traditions of the fathers.

By contrast, Christians and especially English Christians do not show up too well. After 1830, a great effort in church building was made. But it was too late; the new working class had already been alienated from the Church, and has never been won back. English Christians overseas have often shown little interest in having a house of God of their own. And now we seem to be making the same mistake all over again. In so many of the new housing estates, everything else is provided for—shops, civic centres and public houses. If the church comes along six or seven years later the people have become accustomed to their ways, and feel no particular need for a church and all it stands for. We might do well to remember the Indian proverb, 'Never build your house in a village where there is no temple.'

Prayer   *O Lord, who canst be worshipped on the hill-tops and in the far places of the sea, and yet didst descend to fill the temple with thy glory, grant that in every habitation of thy servants there may be visible temples adorned with the beauty of holiness, and a spiritual temple of worshippers adorned with thy Holy Spirit, through Jesus Christ our Lord. Amen.*

Haggai 1, v. 12 to 2, v. 9 (1, v. 1 to 2, v. 9)

When we come to the little prophecy of Haggai, we meet with part of the Old Testament (and this, as we have seen, is rather rare) which can be quite accurately dated. All these prophecies fall within a few months of the second year of King Darius, that is between August and December of 520 BC.

The circumstances are equally clear. Sixteen years before, the Jews had laid the foundation-stone of the temple—and then done little more. Poverty, bad harvests, opposition from relentless enemies had gradually reduced them to a state of discouragement, apathy and worldliness. Haggai has little to say about the great moral principles with which the earlier prophets had dealt; he is concerned with one thing and one thing only—that the temple should be built. This may seem a rather external and inferior concern; but for the moment it was the supremely urgent one. Haggai in his time was quite right, and for two reasons.

What the people needed, to lift them out of their hopelessness and lethargy, was achievement. Modern psychology has confirmed this approach. It is the basis of all rehabilitation work: give a backward child or one who has been mentally ill something that he can do and do well. The pride of achievement works miracles of new life.

Secondly, it was essential that the life of the people should have a visible spiritual centre to hold them together. There was now no monarchy: the law of God and the worship of the temple were the only things left to them. Haggai's brilliant visions, of a shaking of the nations and of future greatness, were not realised at the time, or in the way that he expected. But the second temple for all that did its work; it held the nation together until better times should come.

To think over *'The Gospel is not a matter of persuasiveness in speech but of splendour in action.' (Ignatius, Epistle to the Romans 3, v. 3 ; AD 110)*

Zechariah 8, vv. 1 to 17 (8, vv. 1 to 23)

Few words occur more often in both Old and New Testaments than 'Fear not'. They are spoken at every crisis in the history of revelation, and to almost every one of the heroes of the faith, from Abraham the father of the faithful (Genesis 15:1) to John the Seer dazzled by the sudden vision of the Risen Christ (Revelation 1 :17). Because the Bible is a religious book, this 'Fear not' is not an expression of confidence in human strength, or of merely human optimism; it is always closely related to the character and activity of God.

So in these dark days of discouragement and infirmity, Zechariah comes with his message of encouragement and hope; and we can see that this message is linked at three essential points to the character of God:

1. As the merciful God (vv. 14–15). It is only of God's goodness that the people have been brought back to their own land; this is evidence that sin has been forgiven, and that now it is God's purpose to be gracious to his people.

2. As the righteous God (vv. 16–17). In all these later prophets there is strong emphasis on the rather prosaic and ordinary duties of man to man and of man to society. It is not that God's goodness is conditioned by man's, but that man cannot receive the gifts that God has in store for him, unless he puts himself in such a moral attitude as makes possible their reception.

3. As the God whose purpose reaches far out beyond Israel (v. 13, 20–23). Israel is not only to be blessed, but to be the means of blessing to all nations.

It is because the prophets' hope was so deeply rooted in God that, in spite of partial disappointments, they really did point forward to him in whom all human hopes have been fulfilled.

To think over   *Modern psychology has shown that more disease is caused by fear (worry, anxiety, etc.) than by anything else. Does the biblical 'Fear not' seem to you relevant to this situation?*

Nehemiah 4, vv. 1 to 18 (4, vv. 1 to 23)

We know practically nothing of the history of the Jews between 538 and 444 BC; it seems likely that they had suffered some new disaster at the hands of the barbarous, semi-Bedouin Edomites east of the Jordan (if this is so, it would explain the intense bitterness against the Edomites expressed in several books of the Old Testament). Nehemiah, a court official of the King of Persia, hears of the sad estate of his people, and makes the heroic decision to cross the desert and to come to their rescue. Under his inspiriting leadership, the people are roused from their apathy, and in fifty-two days the wall of Jerusalem is put in defensible condition.

The invention of cannon made a major revolution in human history. Castles are now museum pieces in our landscape; and it takes a great effort for us to imagine what it meant to people in earlier days to have a walled city to which to retreat. Very few such cities fell before assault, though many were captured by starvation or through treachery. Nothing else, in a troubled world, could give an equal sense of security.

In the unconscious self-portraiture of his admirable memoirs, Nehemiah comes before us as a man capable of outstanding powers of leadership, marked by single-mindedness, magnanimity, courage, tact, humility, and above all by a profound faith in God. He was not called to the highest form of ministry. Profoundly convinced (and rightly, for that time) that the Jews could survive only if they were resolutely careful of their racial and religious purity, he was opposed to any alliance with the half-heathen Samaritans of the northern kingdom. In his days, Judaea was a tiny area, and long continued to be so; that it survived at all was largely due to Nehemiah, who thus rightly takes his place in the long chain of witnesses who made ready the way for the coming of the true King of the Jews.

Practical work   *At the Confirmation of the writer of these notes, the text of the sermon was Nehemiah 4, v. 9. Can you reconstruct what the heads of the sermon are likely to have been?*

Daniel 7, vv. 9 to 18 (7, vv. 1 to 28)

In this chapter we find what is to become the familiar symbolism of apocalyptic. The kingdoms of the world are seen as wild beasts, fierce and strong. We have already met Egypt, Assyria, Babylon and Persia; Greece and Rome are yet to come—and then how many more kingdoms of force across the ages. Each seems invincible; but what has been built up by force can be destroyed by force, and in the end is so destroyed! But there is another kingdom, which is built not on force, but on the wisdom of God; and such a Kingdom cannot be destroyed. 'One like unto a son of man' means just 'a man'; the humane kingdom of God's law is thus contrasted with the powers of violence. But in v. 18 'the man' is identified with 'the saints of the Most High'; and that means Israel—Israel at its last gasp in its struggle with Antiochus Epiphanes, yet still in the centre of the picture, still the people to whom the Kingdom is promised.

Such confident sense of vocation can lead and has led to pride, to exclusiveness, to a very ugly nationalism. We all know the little poem:

> How odd
> Of God
> To choose
> The Jews.

Very odd. Odder still that such a people should have had this unchanging conviction that they were the chosen people of God. Oddest of all that *they should have been right.* None of the books of the other ancient religions is in the least like the Old Testament; in broken and scattered lights, as we have seen, it is the revelation of the true God. It was among the Jews that Jesus was born.

And he constantly spoke of himself by the puzzling title, 'the Son of Man'. Probably this term was drawn from several sources; but among them this chapter was perhaps the most important. The Kingdom that Jesus came to bring in is the Kingdom of the righteousness of God: and because of that 'his dominion is an everlasting dominion'.

Prayer *Lord, we adore the mystery of thy working in the past, as thou hast revealed it to us through the Spirit of prophecy: and we pray thee through that same Spirit to grant us understanding that we may discern thy working in the perplexities and confusions of this present age; through Christ our Lord.   Amen.*

☐ So far we have, to a large extent, been following the outward experience of Israel in the changing fortunes of its history—though in Israel history and interpretation are so closely linked that it is never possible completely to separate them. But a large part of the Old Testament is pure poetry, in reading which we come near to the secrets of the inner life of a people in its quest for God and in its relationship to him.

Greatest of all is the great collection of the Book of Psalms. Very few of the Psalms can be accurately dated. The earliest may be as early as the time of David, the latest probably belong to the Maccabean age in the 2nd century BC. Many of the Psalms are closely connected with the worship of the Temple, and show us that that worship was no mere formal round of sacrifices, but that it was linked to some of the deepest experiences of the people, whether as individuals or as a nation. We find here the expression of every possible aspect of religious experience: from despair, conflict, profound penitence, through philosophic questioning to hope, and thence, through quiet confidence in God to the highest expressions of pure praise and adoration. The Psalms have always been the Prayer Book of the Christian Church; if we wish to learn to pray, there is no better method than to study the Psalms carefully, and to use them as the expression of personal devotion.

The Book of Job remains a mystery. None can say by whom it was written or where or when. It is a desert book, and seems to belong to the country east of Jordan; it may have been written in the 7th century BC, though many scholars would place it later. It deals with the age-old problem of suffering. Job passionately fights against the conventional opinion that suffering is always a judgment on sin, and that, because he has so greatly suffered, he must be a specially great sinner. No final answer is given to this question—that had to wait for the Cross and Resurrection of Jesus Christ; but he is left with the humbling and reassuring vision of a God who watches over all his creation and cares for it.

Finally there is the Wisdom literature (Proverbs, etc.). Every simple people lives by its proverbs; know the proverbs and you have the golden key to the psychology of the people. Very often what proverbs express is a kind of prudential, bourgeois morality ('Handsome is as handsome does,' etc.); and there is a great deal of this in the later book of Ecclesiasticus, to be found in the Apocrypha. But the Jews of the Old Testament were not like that; they could not keep God out of any part of their life. So the motto even of the Book of Proverbs is 'the fear of the Lord is the beginning of wisdom'; he is the guardian of conduct and social morality as well as of worship. Amid much that is banal (and a rather severe code for the upbringing of children!), there are many golden utterances of trust in God and of obedience to his will.

Psalm 16, vv. 1 to 11

Nothing in the Old Testament is more remarkable than the absence of any clear hope of eternal life. The Jews, like the Greeks, believed that men continue to exist after death in the gloomy shadow-world of Sheol. But this cannot be called *life*; and in Sheol a man is cut off for ever from the living presence of God. The ordinary view is that 'the dead praise not the Lord, neither any that go down into silence' (Psalm 115:17). The place of the hope of personal immortality is taken by the idea of the survival of the nation; and it is only at the very end of the Old Testament, when the individual comes to be regarded as more important, that the hope of personal survival comes to expression.

Psalm 16 helps us to see the beginning of revelation in this matter. The Bible does not teach 'the natural immortality of the soul'; that was a Greek idea. It does teach that the fellowship of the human soul with God is something that cannot be touched by the death of the body. How far the hope of the writer of this Psalm extended it is difficult to say. He has trusted in God, and yet has been allowed to pass through a time of deep and terrible trouble. He cannot believe that this is the last word, and that his sense of separation from God is to have no end. It may be that his hope did not extend beyond the restoration of God's favour in this life. But the Apostles were right in quoting this Psalm as evidence for the Resurrection of Jesus Christ (Acts 2:25 ff.; 13:35); for to them his resurrection was neither a natural event, nor a kind of magic—it was the consequence of the perfect and unfailing fellowship of Jesus with God.

Prayer *O Lord, help us not to be unduly weighed down either by present troubles or by anxious thought for the future; but to make it our principal concern to remain in constant fellowship with thee, after the example of thy blessed Son, our Lord.*   Amen.

Psalm 50, vv. 1 to 23

From among the many splendid Psalms that might have been chosen, this has been selected for our reading, because it is unlike the majority of the Psalms, in which man is found speaking to God: here it is God himself who is represented as speaking to man. This brings the Psalm very close to the witness of the prophets. Here are the same themes —a vision of God in the sanctuary: criticism of the sacrificial system taken as the be-all and end-all of religion; judgment on the hypocrites, who think that the profession of piety will cover their misdeeds. All this is familiar in the prophets. But perhaps the Psalm goes even further; it seems to lead on to a time when the sacrificial system will not simply be purged of abuses, but will be completely irrelevant, because men will have learned to worship God in quite a different way (vv. 14–15). 'Thou thoughtest that I was altogether such an one as thyself' (v. 21). That is at the very heart and root of man's sin. He makes God in his own image—and so he tries to make use of God for his own advantage. He thinks that God can be hoodwinked by specious piety, or bought off by sacrifices when his honour has been affronted. We all do it—and that is idolatry. The great safeguard against such idolatry is to soak ourselves in the Scriptures, since here God is presented as he really is—the high and lifted up, the Holy One. When confronted with such a God, what can men do but humbly adore and unconditionally obey?

Prayer *Grant, O Lord, that our petitions may always be for those things that may fit us to please thee, and not for such as may be fittest to please ourselves; and, for an accumulation of blessings, so influence our souls with thy divine Spirit, that thy will may ever be our pleasure.* Amen.

Psalm 51, vv. 1 to 17

This wonderful Psalm has been for many centuries the classic Christian expression of sorrow for sin. Traditionally it is associated with David's repentance after his sin with Bathsheba; but probably it dates in reality from a considerably later period, when the sense both of sin and of God's mercy had deepened. There may be times at which the expression of the Psalm may seem to us exaggerated; is sin really as bad as all that? When we say the Confession in the Communion Service, we do not always feel that 'The remembrance of them is grievous unto us; the burden of them is intolerable'; but it is not a question of our feelings: this is a straight, objective state-ment of fact—the burden of our sins is heavier than we can carry of ourselves.

Three points may be noted in the Psalm:

1. The penitent man is not concerned to get off the consequences of his sin, he wants to be clean (v. 7). This is the terrible thing about sin—the stain it leaves: and of that we can never by our own efforts be free.

2. It is on the mercy and faithfulness of God that the penitent relies. (In v. 1 we find again the word *chesed* that we have learned to know in Hosea.) He never changes: and therefore even when we have sinned we can turn again to him with hope.

3. Forgiveness is not granted to the sinner in order to make him feel comfortable inside. The purpose of it is witness (vv. 13–15). If we know that we have sinned and that we have been restored, then we really have something to tell other people about.

Prayer *Almighty qnd everlasting God, who hatest nothing that thou hast made, and dost forgive the sins of all them that are penitent : Create and make in us new and contrite hearts, that we worthily lamenting our sins, and acknowledging our wretchedness, may obtain of thee, the God of all mercy, perfect remission and forgiveness ; through Jesus Christ our Lord.* Amen. (Collect for Ash Wednesday)

Psalm 72, vv. 1 to 19

This is one of the many royal Psalms in the collection. The old title (not part of the original Psalm) is 'To Solomon'. This does not necessarily mean that the Psalm was written in Solomon's time; more likely it is a later and idealised picture of that state of peace and prosperity which was believed to have existed in the days of Solomon. Three features are to be specially noted:

1. The King is represented as receiving the law of his kingdom from God (v. 1). This idea is not unique in Israel; many other monarchs of the ancient kingdoms are represented in the same way as receiving the law from their god.

2. The law of this kingdom is a law of mercy, demanding the protection of the weak and helpless. It is in this especially that the sovereignty of the king is seen. We may here be reminded of what we have read of the Law of Compassion in Deuteronomy.

3. Because of the righteousness of this kingdom, universal dominion is promised to it 'unto the ends of the earth' (v. 8).

It is important to note that this promise is quoted in Zechariah 9:10 —and in the verse before is the reference to the king who is 'lowly, and riding upon an ass, even upon a colt the foal of an ass', which our Lord took up and fulfilled in his triumphal entry into Jerusalem. Clearly he had seen in Psalm and prophecy a picture of the kind of kingdom that he had come to bring in.

In actual fact, wherever the will of Jesus is obeyed, what comes into existence is at least a reflection of the Kingdom as it is shown to us in this Psalm, *1.* in total dependence upon God and upon his orders, *2.* in loving service of the weak and the oppressed, *3.* in universal extension.

Prayer *Lord, may the coming of thy kingdom be our chief concern; and may thy Spirit so cleanse us of all earthly and unworthy thoughts that we may be the servants of such a kingdom as thou canst acknowledge as thine own. Amen.*

Psalm 103, vv. 1 to 22

Much of the best theology in the Old Testament is to be found in the Book of Psalms; but this is primarily the book of the *praises* of Israel, and before we leave it, it is good that we should read one Psalm of pure praise.

For the God of Israel is a glorious God. What is glory? It may be thought of as light or as splendour, but more often in the Bible it is conceived in terms of the flashing forth in action of the tremendous energy of God. In early times this is thought of in rather primitive fashion, as God is heard riding in triumph across the sky in the thunderstorm; later, with a more developed theology, he is the king who holds all the nations in the hollow of his hand; but principally and always he is the God who is active in and for the redemption of his people.

So we find three grounds for the praise that God's people offer to him:

1. His faithfulness. He has chosen a people, and he will not cast them off; as he was in the days of Moses, so he is today.

2. Mercy. His people are sinful, but he will find means to bring them back to himself.

3. Hope. God will be the same in the future as he has been in the past. Man fades and passes away, but God stands fast, and his covenant will endure for ever.

So the end of the Psalm brings us back from earth to heaven, the scene of God's unchallenged authority, of perfect service and unqualified obedience, the place where, in a striking phrase of an earlier Psalm 'in his temple every thing saith, Glory' (29:9). To that place it is the aim of all worship to lead us.

To think over *Look at some of the hymns of praise in our hymn books, and consider how many of them are derived directly from the Book of Psalms.*

Job 3, vv. 1 to 26 (1, v. 1 to 3 v. 26)

Here is the old, old problem: Why should men suffer, and why should I, out of all men, have been called to suffer so beyond all measure?

The story is that Job is a rich and virtuous man who by a series of sudden disasters loses wealth and children and all that he has. Under these shocks Job stands up well; but this is followed by painful, unsightly, and mentally depressing sickness, and then Job gives way—not to the point of repudiating his faith in God, but to the point of despair, and an angry questioning of the justice of God, who can allow such things to happen in this world.

In today's readings we meet Job at one of his lowest points. And this is a terribly faithful picture of what really can happen to human beings. There is suffering, physical and mental, so terrible that it strikes at the very roots of life itself. The sufferer is for the time being far beyond the reach of any consolation of God or man. The whole horizon is dark, and there seems to be no reason why it should ever be anything else. Even the thought of life after death is horrible, because the idea of life has become so inextricably bound up with that of suffering.

Happily not many human beings are called to descend into the same deep pit as Job. But Christianity, if it is true, must have a message for 'all sorts and conditions of men', in whatever situation they may be called to glorify God. To the Christian it is an immense consolation, even if he knows that he cannot fully understand the words, that Jesus on the Cross cried out: 'My God, my God, why hast thou forsaken me?' but went on to say 'Father, into thy hands I commend my spirit.'

Prayer *In the midst of life we are in death; of whom may we seek for succour, but of thee, O Lord? ... O God most mighty, O holy and merciful Saviour ... suffer us not, at our last hour, for any pains of death, to fall from thee.* (Burial service)

Job 5, vv. 17 to 27 (5, vv. 1 to 27)

The greater part of the Book of Job is made up of Job's discussion with his three friends who have come to console with him. From this comes the familiar phrase 'Job's comforters'—those who come with easy speeches but have no real consolation to offer. This is not quite fair to Job's friends. They are good and earnest men, who believe in God. The trouble is that their minds cannot move outside the conventional pattern—virtue brings prosperity, misfortune is the sign of God's displeasure against sin. This is the point of view that, with varying degrees of gentleness and acerbity, they press upon Job. But this means that the real problem of suffering is evaded and not faced.

Today's reading is one of the most beautiful passages in the Bible, and that means that it is one of the most beautiful pieces of writing in the literature of the world, but for all that it is not the word of God. It is an exquisite picture of the man who is at peace with God and with himself and with his own people and with his surroundings. But supposing that all that is taken away and for no explainable reason? Eliphaz then has nothing left to say.

Far too much Christian preaching today, as always, is of this superficial and conventional type.

We have much to learn from our German friends. When the blizzard of Hitler swept over country and church in 1933, they found that all flimsy defences were swept away, and that conventional Christian phrases no longer meant anything. The only thing that mattered was the knowledge of a crucified and risen Saviour.

To think over *One of the hardest tasks is that of writing letters to friends who have been bereaved. What kind of letters do you write when this duty comes your way?*

Job 38, vv. 1 to 21 (38 and 39)

The long debate is at an end. Man at length is still and God is heard to speak. At intervals during the discussion, indications have been given of the thunderstorm looming up over the plain; now it breaks in tropical intensity, and man is revealed in his nakedness and helplessness. Job is convicted of ignorance and arrogance in his attempt to maintain his cause against the splendour and majesty of God.

If possible, the whole of this magnificent poem should be read. In a series of unforgettable pictures it paints for us the wisdom and the wonder of God in creation—first in the inanimate world of wind and rain and snow; then in the animal kingdom in its beauty, its grace, its swiftness, its strangeness, its strength, its terror—wild ass, ostrich, war-horse, crocodile and the rest. Some have interpreted all these as meaning no more than that Job is overwhelmed and crushed by a power which there is no gainsaying: God is God, and man is man, and that is all that is to be said. But is this really so? 'The eyes of all wait upon thee; and thou givest them their meat in due season,' we read in one of the Psalms (145:15). Is not that also the picture here—of a God who delights in the beauty of the world that he has made, who cares for these creatures of his hand, and watches over them? And, if he cares for the wild ass in the trackless paths of the desert, how much more for the sons of man?

This can be no more than a provisional answer since the Old Testament raises far more questions than it can answer. But cannot the message of the Book of Job be summed up in our Lord's words to St Peter: 'What I do thou knowest not now; but thou shalt understand hereafter'? (John 13:7).

To think over   *'Beauty is God's surprise in nature, and the Cross is God's surprise in revelation.'*   (Bishop Winnington-Ingram.)

Job 42, vv. 1 to 6 (42, vv. 1 to 17)

The last eleven verses of the Book of Job are in prose, and give a typical fairy-story ending to the tale. It is probable that this ending is later than the book itself, or it may have been put in by the original author as a kind of consolation prize for those who could not take the strong meat of the great poem. But of course the real ending is in 42:1–6.

At last Job is face to face with God, and not with his own ideas or images of God. The result is just what we have already met with in the vision of Isaiah; whenever man meets with the living God, he is overwhelmed by a sense of utter unworthiness and sinfulness. Job is not here coming round to the viewpoint of his friends, and admitting himself to be guilty of some particularly heinous sin. It is just that he is a son of Adam, and has repeated Adam's primal sin of wanting to make himself independent of God, in fact to be God in his own world.

The great Danish thinker Kierkegaard once wrote a treatise called: 'The blessedness of knowing that before God man is always in the wrong.' Paradox must not be taken too literally, but experience confirms Kierkegaard's insight that there is no greater relief in the world than abandonment of pretence and self-deceiving, and the quiet unemotional, dispassionate recognition that one is a sinner. If to this is added what Job did not know, the truth that God loves sinners, and that there is a welcome for prodigal sons, then the bitterness of humiliation is only the gateway to unending joy.

Prayer *Lord, help us to know ourselves as we are, to see ourselves as we are in thy sight, and also in hope to see ourselves as we shall be, when thou hast finished thy work in us, through Jesus Christ our Lord.* Amen.

Proverbs 8, vv. 1 to 17 (8, vv. 1 to 36)

At the beginning of the Book of Proverbs we find a number of extraordinary, eloquent speeches put into the mouth of wisdom. The
Greeks also sought after wisdom, and we can learn a great deal by
comparison of the Greek with the Hebrew idea. Where shall wisdom
be found? The answer of the Greek sage was, 'Know thyself', look
within—that is where all the secrets of true wisdom are to be found.
So this is a purely human wisdom. Some of the later wisdom books
of the Jews (as we find them in the Apocrypha) had come much
under Greek influence; but here in Proverbs we find the Hebrew
concept in its purity. Wisdom here is always *the wisdom of God.* There
is no encouragement at all in the Bible for introspection. Would you
be wise? Look earnestly at God, especially as he is revealed in Jesus
Christ. Man does not know the depths of the heart of man. God alone
knows what is in man, so look earnestly in the Word of God and you
will find that it is a most unflattering mirror in which you can see just
what you are, and what through Christ you can become. This is the
wisdom, the beginning of which is the fear of the Lord.

Wisdom speaks here so personally as to seem almost a personifica-
tion of God, and we might have expected to find the wisdom idea at
work in the development of the doctrine of the Trinity. In fact this idea
(and especially Proverbs 8:22) did play a considerable part in later
Christian thought. But in the New Testament it is *Jesus Christ* who is
made unto us wisdom from God (1 Cor. 1:30); the less personal idea
of wisdom is completely swallowed up in the fully personal idea of the
Son.

Prayer *O Everlasting wisdom, stretch forth thine hand to us who cannot without thee
come to thee, and reveal thyself unto us, who seek nothing beside thee, through Jesus Christ
our Lord.* Amen.

BETWEEN OLD AND NEW

☐ The Old Testament is a puzzling book. It may be hoped that the reader has by now found some clues through it, and that its magnificent panorama is beginning to take shape. But many perplexities may yet be left; so, before we pass on to the comparatively simple fields of the New Testament, it may be well for the moment to leave all these perplexities in the hands of God, the true God. A very wise man wrote this prayer:

In times of doubt and questioning when our belief is perplexed by new learning, new teaching, new thought, when our faith is strained by creeds, by doctrines, by mysteries beyond our understanding, give us the faithfulness of learners and the courage of believers in thee; give us boldness to examine, and faith to trust all truth; patience and strength to master difficulties; stability to hold fast our traditions with enlightened interpretation, to admit all fresh truth made known to us, and in times of trouble to grasp new knowledge and to construe it loyally and honestly with the old. Save us and help us, we humbly beseech thee, O Lord. Amen.

The New Testament is only about a quarter the length of the Old, and in some ways less perplexing, since it has one simple and evident centre, Jesus Christ. We may find that in the end it leads us into deeper problems, and faces us with sharper challenges. But at the first approach there is much that will speak directly and unconditionally to our hearts.

We find it natural that the New Testament should begin with the Gospels—first the facts about Jesus of Nazareth, then the explanations in the Epistles and other books. It is most important, however, to remember that the order of writing was almost exactly the opposite of this, and that in most cases it can be taken for granted that Epistles came first and Gospels after. We can divide the first century of the Church's history, during which the New Testament was written, roughly into four periods:

AD 29–49. *The period of no writing.*
Christians were telling and retelling the Gospel story. But they were so busy with missionary work, and expected the return of Christ in Glory to take place so soon, that there seemed no special point in writing things down. There may have been some short writings; but nothing has survived from that period in the form in which it was written.

AD 49–69. *The period of letter-writing.*
The earliest New Testament Books are Paul's letters to the Thessalonians (or perhaps Galatians), which date from about AD 50. All Paul's letters were written in the next fifteen years, and perhaps also 1 Peter and James, though the dates of these letters are less certain. Here theology is being poured out red-hot, not thought out in the study, but written urgently to Churches in need of a deeper understanding of the faith, or of guidance as to how to live Christianly in a non-Christian world.

AD 69–89. *The period of history writing.*
In AD 67–70 came the frightful catastrophe of the war between the Jews and the Romans and the destruction of Jerusalem. From that time on the Church had no local centre; the original eye-witnesses were rapidly dying out, and the Lord had not come back. It became

necessary to write down the essentials of the Gospel story as the Church was to proclaim it till the end of the world. The Gospels are not ordinary history; they are a confession of faith, a challenge to faith and a missionary manual.

MARK, the earliest Gospel, seems to have been associated with the Church in Rome. It depicts Jesus as *the Servant of the Lord*, and is in the main a record of what he did and suffered.

LUKE, the Gospel for the Gentiles, shows him as *the Son of Man, the Friend of Sinners*. Renan called this the most beautiful book ever written. Certainly in tenderness and human sympathy it surpasses the other Gospels.

MATTHEW comes from a Jewish background. It shows Jesus as *the King of the Jews*, the fulfilling of Old Testament prophecy; but at the same time it is a Church Gospel, since the Church is the new Israel; and a stark and harsh challenge to a Church which was in danger of losing its first love. It was perhaps written in Syria.

AD 89–100. *The period of thinking things over.*
To this belong the great group of Johannine writings—the Gospel and Epistles of John and the Revelation (not all by the same author). St John's Gospel is not history in any ordinary sense of the term. It is a profound historical meditation on the meaning of the life and death of Jesus, seen in the light of eternity and of God's eternal purpose.

Not all the New Testament books have been fitted into this scheme —of a good many the date is uncertain. But this will serve as a general ground plan, to be borne in mind throughout.

It must always be remembered that the New Testament is the book of the Church. It was written 'from faith to faith', by men who believed in Jesus to other men and women who believed in him, to help them to believe more deeply and to live more truly. We have every right to come to it critically and from without, but, if we do so, we must realise that we are likely to miss a great deal of what the words meant to those who originally read them. Even if we do not yet believe, it will greatly help to put outselves, by imagination and sympathy, as nearly as we can in the position of those first readers. Then we shall be able to understand what it is all about, and understanding may lead us to honest faith.

THIRD MONTH

DAY 1   THE ANGELS' SONG

Luke 2, vv. 1 to 20 (2, vv. 1 to 40)

This is perhaps the best-known passage in the whole Bible. Every Christmas brings it round again, and every child knows 'While shepherds watched their flocks by night'. The result is that we tend to read the record in such a sentimentalised fashion that we may easily fail to see what it is all about. Certainly there are elements of poetry and imagination in the story; but, if we will take the trouble to look behind the form to the content, we shall find that all the great ideas of the New Testament are brought together in this introduction to the life of our Lord. Let us look at only three of them:

1. The message is given to shepherds, i.e. it is a message to the poor. Jesus himself gave it as one of the signs of the Kingdom that the Gospel was being preached to the poor (Matthew 11:5). The true Gospel is always a revolutionary message about the mighty being put down from their seats, and the poor hear it gladly. In India today three-quarters of the Christians are of outcaste origin, from the very poorest and most despised section of the population.

2. This is a message of great joy. Somehow we have managed to give the impression that Christianity is a repressive and gloomy business. It was not so in the beginning. Joy comes in almost every page of the New Testament. The early Christians were bubbling over with 'joy unspeakable and full of glory' (1 Peter 1:8), and had to invent new words to express their feelings.

3. This is a message about a Saviour. So often we give to the word 'Salvation' a sentimental and individual connotation as in the question 'Are you saved?' But look back to Second Isaiah—it is God himself who is the Saviour, the mighty Deliverer, who in a tremendous conflict overthrows his enemies and set his people free. Because Jesus has come, the whole world is being set free from the power of the Enemy.

Luke 2, vv. 40 to 52

This unique and precious episode is our only clue in the Gospels to the development of Jesus between his birth and the beginning of his ministry.

The first visit to Jerusalem must have been a tremendous experience for a Jewish boy (the Jewish ceremony which a little resembles our Confirmation seems in some cases at least to have been carried out at this time) and especially to a boy brought up, as Jesus was, in a pious home and steeped in the literature of the Old Testament. Every place and almost every building would have its historical associations.

Some have found fault with Jesus, saying that his attitude and conduct towards his parents showed lack of sympathy and understanding. Perhaps this is because the critics have not studied the way in which twelve-year-old boys behave, and have not taken seriously the truth that Jesus was really a boy like other boys (apart from sin) and had to learn by experience just as we all have had to do. One of the most notable characteristics of that age is precisely its capacity to become completely absorbed in one thing at a time to the exclusion of all others. And the boy usually takes it for granted that the mind of his elders will work in the same way as his own. 'Where have you been?' The boy is quite surprised at the question; surely the parents can answer the question themselves without asking it!

What is important is the subject in which Jesus was found so enthralled as to have forgotten his separation from his parents. Either the translation, 'In my Father's house' or, 'About my Father's business,' is possible, and the meaning is much the same. That which was to be his overmastering concern till the end of his life has already taken complete possession of his spirit.

To think over   *In the light of the above, consider the saying that 'the Church has usually found it easier to believe in the perfect Godhead of Jesus Christ than to believe in his perfect manhood.'*

Luke 3, vv. 21 and 22 ; 4, vv. 1 to 15

Clearly this story of the temptation must come from Jesus himself; it gives us in poetic and dramatic form some of his deepest thoughts about his ministry.

Each temptation can be related both to Jesus in himself, and to Jesus as the herald of the Kingdom:

I

1. He must not use his great powers for his own comfort or advantage.

2. He must seek no personal power for himself. He who would be a ruler in the Kingdom of God must make himself the servant of all.

3. No spiritual adventures! He must obey the rules, act prudently and take no unnecessary risks.

II

He must not manipulate the motives by which men are most easily and unworthily swayed:

1. Desire for economic security and comfort.

2. Love of a strong leader and admiration for authority.

3. Excitement, specially in relation to that which seems to be supernatural.

There is a good side to all these things; it is the will of God that all men should have enough to eat, that life should be orderly and that it should be interesting. You can see in the Gospels how Jesus was aware of the good side of all these things. But, if we make any of these things an end in itself, we shall end up in chaos. The only true end of man is the Kingdom of God; when we truly and sincerely seek that, all these things will be added to us (Matthew 6:33).

For meditation *'We have not an high priest that cannot be touched with the feeling of our infirmities; but one that hath been in all points tempted like as we are, yet without sin.'* (*Hebrews 4, v. 15*)

Mark 2, vv. 1 to 12

The two words that keep appearing in the records of the life of Jesus are *authority* and *power*. This power was shown both in his words and in his deeds. It was more immediately evident in his deeds, so we will start by considering some of the mighty works that are commonly called 'miracles'.

What is a miracle? In the Christian sense, a miracle is not simply an extraordinary event that defies the usual canons of explanation. Jesus steadily refused to be a mere wonder-worker. In Nazareth, where the people had little faith he could not do many mighty works (Mark 6:5) and when the flippant King Herod desired to see a miracle done by him, he was disappointed (Luke 23:8). To Jesus miracles are evidence that in him the Kingdom of God is at work, and the aim of this Kingdom is the restoration of all men's powers to that which in the beginning God intended them to be. For this reason, inner healing through the restoration of a right relationship to God is more important than the healing of the body. This comes out clearly in today's reading. Jesus does not say that all sickness is due to sin, or that this particular man's sickness is due to his sins. But the command, 'Take up thy bed and walk' is given only after the affirmation, 'Son, thy sins are forgiven.'

This raises the vital question as to which of these two sayings is the harder. To outward appearances it is the latter, since no one can *see* whether forgiveness has taken place or not, whereas everyone can see whether the sick man really rises up and walks or not. To Jesus it is not so; the reality of forgiveness can be answered only through the tremendous conflict of the Cross; in comparison with this everything else is secondary and easier. Only if we have understood this fundamental principle can we make sense of the record of the life of Jesus.

Prayer *Lord, give us grace that, while desiring the healing of all our bodily ills, we may desire more earnestly the healing of our spirits, through the redemption that is in thy Son, Jesus Christ our Lord.* Amen.

Mark 5, vv. 1 to 20

Many events in the life of Christ are set forth in terms of a conflict with the demons. No one who has lived close to the people in a non-Christian country is likely to doubt the terrible reality of an invisible, active power of evil. No Christian is likely to doubt that the life of Jesus was the culminating point in the struggle between good and evil in the world. But it does not follow that we, with our more scientific understanding of health and sickness, are bound to accept every detail of the accounts as given in the Gospels.

In today's extraordinarily vivid reading, it seems that our Lord was dealing with a man whom today we would call insane. The madman, in his intense desire to be rid of his sickness, runs towards the herd of swine shouting and waving his arms, and easily starts the panic which sends the swine careering down the steep slope to their death in the waters of the lake.

This is not the important part of the story. The important points are:

1. That a man whose mind had been troubled and clouded by sickness is restored to wholeness and soundness of mind.

2. That the man wanted to stay close by Jesus.

3. That this was not allowed but the man was sent to be a witness for Christ to his own people.

In these three sentences are summoned up the whole experience and mission of the Church.

To think over   *Do you agree that we are entitled to explain certain things in the Gospels in modern terms ; or does it seem to you that by doing so we explain them away ?*

Luke 7, vv. 1 to 10 (7, vv. 1 to 17)

There are several interesting points in today's reading.

This belongs to a small class of miracles of healing at a distance. Usually Jesus healed only those who were personally present before him; but sometimes the faith of fathers or friends was allowed to take the place of the faith of the persons most concerned; and in such cases distance seems to have been no obstacle to the going forth of our Lord's healing power.

Secondly, this is one of the few recorded examples of a miracle performed for the benefit of a Gentile. During his earthly ministry our Lord confined himself strictly to a mission to the Jews; it was only after the Resurrection that this mission was extended to all the world. But there were exceptions; certain Gentiles showed by their faith that in spirit at least they belonged to the chosen people ; and for them their faith availed no less than for the Jews.

Thirdly, though perhaps we ought not to press the centurion's words too hard, they do constitute a very remarkable confession of faith. He shows a close parallel between his own position and that of Jesus, since each is exercising not a personal but a delegated authority. Jesus can do these great works, because he is invested with the power of his Father to whom he is perfectly obedient. This is exactly what Jesus said of himself; in the Fourth Gospel occur several times the words: 'Of myself I can do nothing'—and just because he could of himself do nothing, he could in fact do all things.

To think over *Why do you think the earthly ministry of Jesus was limited only to the Jews?*

Matthew 11, vv. 1 to 15 (11, vv. 1 to 25)

A great many people were asking the same question as John the Baptist; was Jesus the promised Messiah or not? In some ways he seemed to be; he was speaking with authority and doing mighty works—on the other hand, there was no denunciation of the Romans, no political movement, no sign of an earthly kingdom. So John sends to ask him a direct question.

The reply of Jesus is typical of his method of teaching. He hardly ever gives a direct answer to a direct question; his method is to say to the questioner: 'You really have all the evidence before you—look around you and use your brains, and you all find that you will already have the answer to your own question.' Here he does give a further hint, since his answers contain allusions to Isaiah 35:5 and 61:1, and so, as we may remember, point to a deliverance far greater than the deliverance of the Jews from Babylonia. But still it is John who must make up his mind.

This is a warning to us. The signs of the Kingdom were all around John and his friends. But, because for the most part they were asking the wrong question, it was very difficult for them to find the right answer. We may so easily do the same. It is very difficult to approach Jesus with an open and unprejudiced mind. The more we are able to do so, the more likely it is that he will help us to formulate the right questions. But even then it is unlikely that he will give us the kind of answer that we seek; we have to work out the answer for ourselves. This is hard, but it is the only way to educate men for freedom; and God will not have any other than free men in his Kingdom.

Prayer   *O Lord, the signs of the Kingdom are all about us, but often we are too blind to see them. Open our eyes that we may see and believe and obey, for Jesus Christ's sake.   Amen.*

Matthew 13, vv. 1 to 9 and 18 to 23 (13, vv. 1 to 23)

We turn now from the mighty works of Jesus to his mighty words. As everyone knows, many of these words were spoken in parables. The Hebrew word so translated is used in a great many senses— riddle, proverb, comparison, and so on. The parables of Jesus mostly fall into one of two classes—short, pointed illustrations from nature, and more fully developed stories from human relationships.

In earlier times there was a tendency to treat the parables as *allegories*, i.e. to think that every detail had some hidden mysterious meaning, and a great deal of ingenuity was expended in trying to work out their meanings. We now see that this was a false way; the details are put in, as every story-teller puts them in, for the sake of realism or vividness; each parable has just one point, one lesson; and in the study of each of them our task is to find out what that one point, that one lesson, is.

The parable of the sower is a parable of *the Kingdom*; its aim is to make clear the nature of the Kingdom by comparison with what happens to the seed when it is sown. The very centre of the mission of Jesus is to make known to men the reality of the Kingdom and the certainty of its coming. So here we can distinguish four stages:

1. The insignificance of the beginning;

2. Many frustrations by the way;

3. The certainty of its coming—harvest does come in due time, though most of the sower's labour may seem to have been wasted;

4. The splendour of the accomplishment, by contrast with the smallness of the beginning.

And implied is the sense of urgency—men must make up their minds whether they will enter into this Kingdom or not.

To think over   *On an honest assessment of ourselves, into which of the four categories of hearers named in the interpretation of the parable do we seem most readily to fit?*

Luke 10, vv. 25 to 37

This is an excellent example of our Lord's teaching method. It has been laid down that the second great commandment is 'Love thy neighbour'; the question is raised: 'Who is my neighbour?' It would have been easy for Jesus simply to say in general terms: 'Everyone is your neighbour.' Instead he tells one of the most brilliant of his parables, and then challenges the lawyer to answer his own question.

Most readers think that the meaning of the parable is: 'Anyone who is in need has a claim upon you; you must regard him as your neighbour.' This is of course true, but is it not to read the parable the wrong way round? The lawyer is *a Jew*. Is not our Lord saying: 'Put yourself in the place of the injured man. Half-conscious, you hear the footsteps approaching and you see the fellow countrymen, on whose help you ought to be able to count, pass you by, the priest because the law forbids him to touch a dead body, the Levite perhaps because he is hurrying on to perform his appointed service in the temple. In such circumstances you quickly discover who is your neighbour; and when a man, on whom you have no claim whatever, stops and pours out help upon you with an exuberance of generosity, you do not stop to ask whether he is clean or unclean, Jew or Gentile, black or white.'

Surely this fits in much better with the parable as actually told by our Lord. And is there perhaps a yet deeper sense behind it; if you come to understand just what the situation of the sinner is in the sight of God, you will begin to realise just what it means that the Son of Man came to seek and to save that which was lost.

Practical work   *Try to write a modern version of the parable in the terms of Israel and the Arabs, or Africa or England today.*

Luke 15, vv. 11 to 32 (15, vv. 1 to 32)

This is perhaps the best known of all the parables of Jesus, and perhaps one of the least understood. It is commonly called the parable of the Prodigal Son; but there are in fact two sons in the parable, and each is as important as the other. Yet many people who know the Bible quite well will find it hard to quote accurately the remarks of the elder son.

Jesus' method of making friends of publicans and sinners by no means commended itself to the religious leaders of the Jews. He is here defending himself against their criticisms, and telling them that, if they had known what God is really like, they would have understood why he acted as he did.

The elder brother is the typical respectable man, who has never done anything particularly wrong. He is full of self-complacent virtue, but without love. In every word he speaks he gives himself away; and the climax comes when he refers to 'thy son' but not to 'my brother' (v. 30). In this strange world, it is certainly dangerous to be bad, but apparently it is even more dangerous to be good!

The younger brother has at least the grace to know that he has sinned. He comes home demanding nothing for himself—and finds himself overwhelmed by the warmth of his reception. (Note the exuberance with which our Lord piles up the manifestation of the father's unchanging love.) This inheritance which he has wasted is gone for good; that can never come back. Many months may pass before he is restored to health, and the scars of the far country are healed. But he is no longer in the far country; he is home, and that is all that matters. And that is what God is like.

To think over *What guarantee has the father that the younger son will not slip back and return to his old evil course?*

Matthew 18, vv. 21 to 35

The forgiveness of sins is one of the blessings which Jesus came to bring and to assure to men. The parable of the Two Sons shows us the unrestrained generosity of God in forgiveness. But God does not just do things to us from outside—there is always the question of the response that man makes to God's initiative.

It is important not to apply all the details of this parable to God: our Lord is describing the way in which kings and great ones in his day acted, and the details make the picture exceedingly vivid. But in the application of the parable only two things matter—the contrast between the enormous debt of the one servant and the trivial debt of the other; and the withdrawal of the forgiveness already granted from the servant who would not forgive.

But does this not make forgiveness into a kind of bargain: 'You forgive your brethren, and then I will forgive you'? This would be a misunderstanding. Christ has given us two great commandments— to love God and to love our brethren—and these two hang together. If we shut ourselves off from our brethren by refusing to forgive them, we shut ourselves off also from God. He is willing to forgive us all the time, but as long as we cut ourselves off from him, his forgiveness cannot take effect in us.

It is not as though we had first to forgive our enemies or our brethren, and then come to God to ask for forgiveness for ourselves. In fact, the order is usually the exact opposite of this. To forgive a really grave injury is the most difficult thing in the world. It is perhaps only the wonder of the fact that in Christ God has forgiven us that makes it possible for us to forgive the one who has done the wrong.

Prayer *Lord, when we have been wronged, and our hearts are sore and resentful, call to our remembrance the price that Christ paid in order that we might be forgiven ; and enable us to forgive our brethren even as thou hast forgiven us.* Amen.

Matthew 25, vv. 31 to 46

This tremendous parable goes a little way to meet our natural question: 'What is to be the fate of those who have never heard the message of the Gospel?' Jesus seems to say, 'They have had plenty of opportunities of meeting me: whenever anyone suffers, I suffer in him; whoever serves the afflicted is always serving me.'

But the application of the parable is severely and alarmingly practical: 'Look to yourselves.' Both groups in the parable have the same opportunities; the only difference was that one lot was blind and the others could see. The charity of the one was not the calculating goodness that expects a reward, but simply the overflowing of a generous heart. The failure of the other was caused not by any exceptional hardness of heart but just by insensitiveness to the claims of human need.

Real Christian faith has always found its expression in patient, loving service of those who are in need. At the same time the Church is capable of the most astonishing blindness. It took a long time to awaken even Christian consciences to the conditions under which chimney sweeps worked a hundred years ago, and to conditions in prisons and lunatic asylums. It is all too easy to say that things cannot happen like that now. Are you sure? Do you *know* exactly how hard it is for a man who has been in gaol to get a job and make a new start in life? To pay a subscription to a charitable organisation is good. But is it enough? Ought not every Christian to have some personal contact with human need, and to take some personal responsibility of service? There is plenty of work to go round!

Prayer *Lord, thou hast so often passed us in the street and we have not known thee. Open our eyes to see thee here, that we may see thee without fear on the day of Judgment.* Amen.

Matthew 5, vv. 1 to 16 (5, vv. 1 to 48)

The parables have given us various pictures of the Kingdom of God. In the forefront of his Gospel, Matthew sets the Sermon on the Mount as a kind of summary of the law of the new kingdom, and an indication of the character that is expected of its citizens.

One sometimes hears people say, 'If only everyone would live by the principles of the Sermon on the Mount'; and one wonders whether they have ever read it. For the Sermon is a terrifying document in the standards that it sets and in the demands that it makes. Note that the Sermon does not consist of moral good advice, which everyone is able to follow, if he wishes.

1. Everything is related to God and to obedience to his will.

2. Everything depends on acceptance of a certain relationship to Jesus Christ.

3. The principles here set out are diametrically opposed to the ideas, ambitions and desires on which human society is ordinarily based.

4. These are commands, and Jesus expects that they will be obeyed.

Today's reading is a prescription for true happiness (the word translated 'blessed' means 'happy'). Happiness is promised to people of a certain character—to those who make no demands for themselves (the poor in spirit); to those who are more concerned about the needs of others than their own (the merciful); to those who cheerfully accept undeserved obloquy and persecution (vv. 10–12).

This is hardly what the world understands by happiness; it is hardly the advice that one would give to a young man setting out to make a success of life. Perhaps Christianity is not quite so simple as people seem to think!

To work out *'Christ demands that we should fulfil the requirements of the Sermon on the Mount. It is quite clear that man cannot fulfil them. Therefore . . .' How should this sentence end?*

Matthew 6, vv. 19 to 24 (6, vv. 1 to 34)

These words are to be taken seriously; and if taken seriously, they may well make us wonder whether we are Christians at all.

'Take no thought for the morrow.' Of course this is not an encouragement for carelessness. The Christian has no business to be casual and inefficient in his job, and like everyone else he must exercise that reasonable foresight without which no job can get done. The words mean 'Take no anxious thought'.

Half the sickness in the world, and perhaps more than half the unhappiness, is caused by anxiety; by worry about the future. Worry makes no contribution to the solution of any problem. And more than that, to the Christian worry is sin, since it is evidence of failure really to believe in God.

Again, this is not meant to encourage a shallow optimisim, as though everything would work out all right for everyone in the end. The negative is balanced by a very important positive: 'Seek ye first the Kingdom of God'—that must be the central and all-controlling aim. To have such a central aim gives life calm and balance and spontaneity. God gives no promises that things will be made easy for those who seek his kingdom, or that they will be kept safe from any of the natural troubles and sorrows of the world: he just gives the promise that he himself is adequate to every situation, and will see us through. Probably every reader of these notes knows at least one person in whose life suffering and sorrow have been transformed by Christian grace into strength and beauty. What others have we may have too—but only on the basis of total and unconditional loyalty to God as revealed in Jesus Christ.

Prayer   *From a divided and anxious mind, Good Lord, deliver us.*

Matthew 7, vv. 13 to 29

The Sermon on the Mount is a dreadfully disturbing document. It faces us with challenge after challenge, from which if we are serious we cannot escape. In these closing verses Jesus presses the challenge home under the figures of the Way, the Fruit and the Rock.

The way of Jesus is a narrow way; to walk in it involves saying No to many natural things—pride, ambition, lust, self-pleasing; but these are no more than the sacrifices that the mountain climber knows that he must make, if he is to attain his goal.

The condition of following Jesus is absolute sincerity, and this is not easy to achieve. It is so easy to think that we can compromise, that we can separate the areas in which we act as Christians from those in which we act like everyone else. It is so easy to make use of religion for our own advantage or comfort that even Christians of many years standing have to be on their guard against this danger.

Jesus is personally the humblest of men; but on his claims as the messenger of God he is adamant. He is the voice of God calling men to obedience; they must decide, and in their decision is involved infinite gain or loss—a house which stands or a house which falls. Of course we are free to say No; but we must accept the judgment which, by saying No, we bring upon ourselves.

Conversion to Christ is only in a tiny degree an emotional experience. It is roughly half understanding and half will. It is a dispassionate consideration of what in general is involved in obedience to Christ, and of what in particular is involved for me. It is an act of the will in which, seeing where the chalk line is drawn on the floor, we quite quietly and deliberately with God's help step across it to the side of Christ.

Of course we can say No, if we want to. And in fact if we have not said a deliberate and irrevocable Yes, we are saying an as yet mercifully revocable No.

To be settled *Yes or No.*

Mark 8, vv. 27 to 38

Today we encounter once again Jesus' method of teaching not by answering questions but by asking them. The point has been reached at which he can put to the disciples the most important question of all: 'Who say you that I am?'

The situation in which the question is asked is most significant. There had been much discussion as to whether Jesus is the Messiah or no. But he had done none of the things that the Messiah was expected to do. He had shown no signs of raising an insurrection against the Romans; he had alienated both the religious and the political leaders among the Jews: when the people wished to make him king, he refused the offer; now he is in fact running away, since the Greek-speaking area of Caesarea Philippi was not part of the Holy Land of Palestine.

This is the situation in which Peter makes his confession, 'Thou art the Christ', and that is what gives it immense importance. He has seen that Jesus must be followed at all costs and unconditionally; if he does not fit in with the traditional ideas of Messiahship, then it is the traditional ideas of Messiahship that must be changed. Peter really is the first believer, and in this sense it is true that he is the rock on which the Church is built (Matthew 16:18).

It is true that this faith is still very rudimentary. Peter is prepared to accept a Messiah who does not fight. He cannot accept the teaching of Jesus that Messiah must suffer. And for all of them, and especially on Good Friday, that was the incredible and intolerable contradiction—that Messiah should suffer. That was because they were still thinking like men, and not thinking as God thinks (v. 33). We are all in the same danger: God's way of working is so completely different from ours that a revolution has to take place in our minds if we are to understand it.

Prayer *Lord, help us not to attempt to fit thee into the pattern of our ideas, but to allow our ideas to be transformed into the perfect pattern thou hast shown us in our Saviour Jesus Christ.* Amen.

Mark 9, vv. 1 to 13 (9, vv. 1 to 29)

Very little is told us in the Gospels of the hidden inner life of Jesus in fellowship with his heavenly Father. It comes out most clearly in the three dramatic occasions when a voice spoke to him from heaven—at his Baptism, just before his Passion (John 12:28) and here in the Transfiguration; at the beginning of his ministry, at the end of it, and here at a central turning-point. Peter has made his confession; the Church is now in existence in embryo; the Son of Man must go up to Jerusalem to face his fiercest conflict and to win his greatest victory. The Transfiguration is in part guidance to Jesus as to the next step that he must take; in part illumination for the disciples to help them through the difficult days that are to come.

The modern reader is likely to miss the point of the story through failure to understand the meaning of 'the cloud' in the Bible. It means the hidden, mysterious glory of God abiding among his people. Moses was not able to enter into the tabernacle, because the cloud abode thereon, and the glory of the Lord filled the tabernacle (Exodus 40:38). At the dedication of the temple, 'the cloud filled the house of the Lord, so that the priests could not stand to minister' (1 Kings 8:10–11). 'Ye shall see the Son of man . . . coming with the clouds of heaven' (Mark 14:62). That which the tabernacle and the temple stood for is now realised and fulfilled in Jesus of Nazareth. This links up with his word to the Jews, 'Destroy this temple, and in three days I will raise it up . . . he spake of the temple of his body' (John 2:19–21). Our faith is directed not to a Place, but to a Person. The old covenant has passed away; we are children of the new covenant of which the essence is the presence and the glory of God in Jesus Christ, abiding with his people for ever.

To think over *Contrast the biblical idea of 'the cloud' with the ways in which the word is often used today—threatening clouds, cloud of gloom, of anxiety, etc.*

Luke 19, vv. 1 to 10

A wise teacher has said, 'If only people could understand that the miracle of Zacchaeus is the great miracle, they would be able to understand the Gospel'.

We have comparatively few records of our Lord's dealings with individuals. That found in today's reading is extraordinarily full of teaching.

Zacchaeus' motive may have been little more than curiosity; but the Lord is willing to enter through the narrowest doors.

Jesus is at once met with the usual criticism. The tax-gatherers were hated because of their association with the Roman power, and because of their greedy and oppressive ways—no fit company for a religious teacher!

Jesus behaves with the courtesy due from a guest; he says nothing about the sinner's sins—nor need we; after all the sinners know a great deal more about them than we do.

Yet the mere presence of Jesus is enough to make Zacchaeus acutely aware of his sins, and anxious to be rid of them.

But repentance cannot be carried out in the abstract; it involves a man's willingness to face himself at his own weakest point.

And repentance is not real, until it finds its expression in practical action, usually at the point at which it will hurt most.

When the invitation of Jesus and genuine repentance come together, the result is what is called salvation (v. 9)—the healing of the soul and the restoration of a right relationship both to God and to other men.

Prayer *Lord, we have little to offer thee except our sins; but, if thou be pleased to turn aside into our house, such welcome as we can give thee shall be thine.   Amen.*

Matthew 21, vv. 1 to 17

The passover, or some other Jewish festival, was approaching and many thousands of pilgrims were streaming in from all the cities and villages of Palestine, and from many other countries as well. Now, if ever, was the moment for Jesus to declare himself. So, this once, he decided to declare himself in public.

It is clear that the 'Triumphal Entry' was not a sudden and spontaneous gesture. Jesus had carefully pondered and planned it. He had read in Zechariah the prophecy: 'Rejoice greatly, O daughter of Zion; shout, O daughter of Jerusalem; behold, thy King cometh unto thee; he is just and having salvation; lowly, and riding upon an ass, even upon a colt the foal of an ass.' This prophecy he determined to fulfil in action. In the Old Testament, the horse is the steed of the warrior, and the mule the steed of the king; it is peaceful travellers, such as merchants, who ride upon asses. So there is in this action of Jesus a paradox; he is a King; but will the people recognise and accept the nature of his kingdom?

Was the Triumphal Entry a 'success' or not? In a way it was; there had been enthusiasm for him among the crowds. But was this really what he wanted? Had they not done their best to turn his entry into the city into the pompous procession of an oriental monarch? What connection was there between this excitement and the quiet obedience to the Will of God, which was what Jesus really demanded?

The contrast is often drawn between the enthusiasm of the crowd on Palm Sunday, and their failure to save Jesus on Good Friday. This was perhaps no more than was to be expected from the usual instability of a crowd. But some did not forget; we may see here a preparation for the extraordinarily rapid growth of the Church after the resurrection.

Extra work   *Find in the hymn book and read the two Palm Sunday hymns: 'All glory, laud and honour,' and 'Ride on, ride on in majesty.'*

Matthew 21, vv. 23 to 32 (21, vv. 23 to 46)

Here is another brilliant example of our Lord's method of answering a question by asking another question.

There are two kinds of authority in the Church—that of the priest and that of the prophet. The authority of the priest comes from God, but is conveyed through the Church in ordination (the Jews had a similar ceremony). The priest has credentials which he can show to anyone who asks him 'By what authority?' and what he says is covered and guaranteed by the authority of the Church. Not so the prophet. He acts under the direct impulsion of the Spirit of God. His message must be self-authenticating; it must stand or fall by its own inner spiritual power, and not by any external guarantee. Anyone can be convinced by the credentials of a priest; it takes a certain spiritual sensitiveness to be able to recognise a prophet. But the questioners were spiritual leaders among the people, and Jesus had a perfect right to put to them the question: 'Did you accept John as a prophet, and did you recognise the source of his power? If so, *a fortiori* you will accept me; and so you have the answer to your own question'.

This is all very relevant to us today. Christian apologetic has often gone off on sidetracks—the long history of Christianity, the good deeds done by Christians, the progress made by Christian countries, and so on. But really the only way to convince ourselves, or anyone else, of the truth of Christ's claims is to expose ourselves directly to the power of his words. If we do so, we are likely to say, like the messengers of the Jews (John 7:46), 'Never man so spake'. If we are perfectly honest and somewhat spiritually sensitive, we are bound to go on and ask: 'Why is this?' In so asking, we really have the answer to our own question.

To think over   *Karl Marx also was a kind of prophet. How do we distinguish a true prophet from a false prophet?*

Matthew 22, vv. 15 to 22 (22, vv. 15 to 46)

Jesus had indeed a difficult path to tread between the Roman power on one hand and the many parties among the Jews on the other; and the question about the tribute money seemed well planned to get him into difficulties whatever answer he gave. If he said that tribute money might be paid, that could be used to discredit him with the fanatically anti-Roman party among the people; if he said that it should not be paid, this could be used to get him into trouble with the Roman authorities.

Jesus, with marvellous skill, walks straight through the trap, and answers the question on a far deeper level than the questioners had expected. There were two kinds of coinage in Palestine, the Roman, in which ordinary business was carried on, and the Jewish which was used only for the purposes of the Temple. The Roman tribute could not be paid in the Jewish coins, and the Temple tax could not be paid in the Roman coin, since it had the emperor's head on it, as this was regarded as a breach of the second commandment. By producing the Roman coin the Pharisees gave away the fact that they too used it for their ordinary business—and thereby contracted certain obligations to the ruling power, in spite of their disapproval of it.

The question of the relationship of Church and State is one for which there is no perfect solution. Every solution has been tried, from complete separation of the two to complete identification of the one with the other. The Christian can recognise that both are gifts from God. Law and order are necessary in society, if men are to live together at all; the other realm, ruled by love and forgiveness, is necessary if men are to rise to the fulness of their being. The Christian can recognise that he has a loyalty to both God and Caesar; on the understanding that if there is a clash between the claims of the State and the claims of God, it is always the higher loyalty that must prevail.

To think over   *Do you regard the present relations between Church and State as satisfactory? If not, in what way do you think they ought to be changed?*

Mark 14, vv. 12 to 26 (14, vv. 1 to 31)

The Holy Communion brings us nearer to Jesus Christ than anything else that we say or do. It is meant to be the Sacrament of unity; unhappily the Churches have fought one another about its meaning. Today let us look simply at the teaching which comes clearly out of the events of the Last Supper itself, and in which all the Churches would probably be agreed.

Jesus had many times eaten with the disciples, and must have often broken the bread and blessed the cup, since this is what the head of a Jewish family regularly did at meal times. But on this occasion he gave a special solemnity to the act, because he knew, as the disciples did not yet grasp, that it would be the last occasion. What did his action mean?

1. This was Passover time; the Jews were commemorating their great deliverance from Egypt in the Exodus; but Jesus had come to bring about a greater deliverance than that.

2. At the Exodus God had made a covenant with his people through Moses; Jesus is inaugurating a new and better covenant, which will bring the gift of the forgiveness of sins.

3. The first covenant was made through the blood of slain animals; the new covenant can be brought in only through the death of the One whom God has sent to establish it.

4. In the first covenant Israel was made one people. So the people of Jesus is one people, but not through any natural relationship, only because each individual is first directly related to Jesus through personal loyalty to him.

5. This is possible only if Jesus is perpetually present with his people as he was at the Last Supper, to renew this personal loyalty to himself.

6. No one should eat of that Bread and drink of that Cup, unless he is prepared to die for his Master, as his Master has died for him. In point of fact, the Church has survived so long only because in each generation there have been enough men and women who were willing to die for Christ.

The Church has, through experience, learned many other meanings of the Eucharist. But if we could, every Sunday, make these six elementary points a reality in our lives, would we not have gone very far in the way of following Jesus?

John 14, vv. 1 to 14 (14, vv. 1 to 31)

So far we have read only from the first three Gospels; now, for some of the deepest lessons of our Lord, we must turn to the Fourth, where we find not so much direct transcription of our Lord's words as deeply thought out interpretation of them. In the three chapters of this last great discourse the disciples are given assurance of the adequacy of our Lord's provision for them, after he has been withdrawn from their sight.

Today's reading centres upon the great sayings, 'I am the way', and 'He that hath seen me hath seen the Father'.

'I am the way.' Jesus does not describe for us the goal, except that he tells us that he is going to the Father. He does not define or describe the way: he simply says 'I am the way'. If we are in the way we need not worry about the goal. And since the way is a person and not a map, the Christian life can never be reduced to rules; it must always be a matter of freedom, of education, of discovery; yet not discovery of the wholly unknown, but deeper discovery of the meaning of him whom we have already known.

'Show us the Father.' Jesus does not describe the Father; he who has seen Jesus needs no other picture or description. The prophets had said, 'Thus saith the Lord'; Jesus says, 'I say unto you'; there is the difference. He comes to lead men to the Father; but in leading them to himself, he *is* leading them to the Father. All that we can know of God is set forth in Jesus Christ. There are many mysteries in God that we cannot know now; to attempt to go beyond what we can see in Jesus Christ is likely to lead us rather into a vague mysticism or pantheism than on to deeper truth. In him God is revealed as a person, one whom we can know and love and serve. In this present life, do we need any more than this?

Prayer *O Almighty God, whom truly to know is everlasting life: Grant us perfectly to know thy Son Jesus Christ to be the way, the truth, and the life; that, following the steps of thy holy apostles, Saint Philip and Saint James, we may steadfastly walk in the way that leadeth to eternal life; through the same thy Son Jesus Christ our Lord. Amen.*

John 15, vv. 1 to 15 (15, vv. 1 to 27)

In Chapter 14, Jesus has assured his disciples, under various figures, that they can count on his continued presence with them, after his return to be with his Father. In this chapter, he adds a new dimension of intimacy to this relationship, by speaking in terms of the vine and the branches. Jesus is the vine, not the stock of the vine; he is, as it were, incomplete without the branches, without those whom he has called into fellowship with himself. We are incomplete without him; we can have no true inner life, if we remain apart from him. St Paul will speak of Christ dwelling in our hearts by faith; of Christ as the Body in which we all are members. What do these remarkable expressions mean?

In sermons, Christ is often presented to us as the Lord in whom we should believe; the Gospel is the law that we should obey; Jesus is the Example, whom we should follow. All this is fine. But such a Lord can seem very remote from us. When we try to obey this law, we find it is too difficult for us; when we try to follow the example of Jesus, we are reduced to despair by the difference between him and us. This chapter offers us quite a different possibility—not of effort, but of growth; of a Jesus who became part of our inner life, so that we may become part of his life.

Countless Christians have borne witness as to the nature of this life. When they have longed after goodness, it was not just a desire of their own, but an inspiration that was given to them. When they understood some new truth, it was not their own wisdom that discovered it—it was light that was given to them. When they overcame sin, or made some difficult decision, it was not their own will that did it, but the power of Another co-operating with their will. It is the living Christ himself who touches life at every point, and becomes part of everyday experience.

To think over   *In what way do you usually think of Christ? What metaphor would most suitably express your experience of him?*

John 16, vv. 1 to 15 (16, vv. 1 to 33)

Jesus has promised his disciples that they will not be left alone to carry on his work. In this chapter he makes it clearer how this will be so—the Comforter will come.

This is a difficult word to explain or translate; Comforter, Advocate, Helper, Strengthener—all these ideas go into it, and none of them exhausts it. Perhaps the best way to explain it is to say that, when the Holy Spirit comes, he will do for the disciples all that Jesus had done for them in the days of his flesh, and would bring to completion that which Jesus had begun.

Here two aspects of his work are specially emphasised:

1. In relation to the world he will vindicate the work and the way of Jesus. That way of weakness and suffering had seemed so foolish; the Holy Spirit will make clear that that really was the way of the victory and the power of God.

2. In relation to the disciples, he will make clear the meaning of all that Jesus had said and done. There was so much that they could not now understand; but they would not be left alone to work it out for themselves, they would have a divine friend and guide.

It must have seemed strange to the disciples that Jesus should have said, 'It is good for you that I go away' (v. 7). Yet so it was. In his earthly life, Jesus was limited to one place and one group of friends. When the Holy Spirit comes, he will be available everywhere and for all people, to do for them at all times all that Jesus had done for his friends. In a sense he will not bring anything new—he will simply bring Jesus—so that we need not go to Jerusalem, or back into the first century to seek him. He is ours here and now.

Prayer　*Come, Holy Ghost, our souls inspire,*
And lighten with celestial fire;
Thou the anointing Spirit art,
Why dost thy sevenfold gifts impart.

Mark 14, vv. 32 to 42 (14, vv. 32 to 72)

The story of Jesus in Gethsemane brings him very near to other men and women who are called to suffer. At the same time it reminds us that there are depths in his character and career which are very hard for us to penetrate. What was the nature of his conflict in the garden?

First, perhaps, his need for certainty. The Gospel makes it clear that he, like us, had to wait for guidance from his heavenly Father. There were so many other possibilities before him. He could return to Galilee, where he would probably be left untroubled. He could go and preach to the Gentiles, who seemed so ready to respond. The answer comes that this is the way that the Father has chosen; there is for him no other way than death.

This being clear, there is, next, the conflict involved in the ready acceptance of death. Jesus was a young man, in the full vigour of manhood. The instinct of self-preservation is the strongest of all instincts. The soldier who engages in a forlorn hope has at least a hope of surviving; here it was a case of going open-eyed to absolutely certain death—and this is possibly only through total self-mastery, and a stern resolution of the will.

Thirdly, there was the bitter question whether his death would be of any avail. The faith of the disciples was still so weak and confused. Could they be relied upon to carry on his work? Would he not be throwing everything away by venturing upon death?

The victory was won, but it was hardly won. What was decided on in Gethsemane had to be carried to its completion in his death on Calvary; but in principle the victory had already been won in the lonely conflict and the consolation of Gethsemane.

Prayer. *Lord, let the doing of thy will be always our chief concern ; and, if the doing of that will should lead us to conflict or suffering, let Gethsemane give us the assurance that suffering for thy sake is never in vain.   Amen.*

Mark 15, vv. 1 to 20

Many mixed motives played their part in the betrayal and trial of Jesus. The leaders of the Jews were determined to be rid of him, because he threatened both their religious and their political power. But they had to persuade Pilate the Governor that he was a menace to Roman rule in Palestine; and the people that he was a deceiver, who had fed them with false hopes that he could not fulfil. In the end the Governor seems to throw the decision back on the people.

Jesus or Barabbas? Barabbas was not an ordinary criminal; he seems to have been the head of one of those terrorist groups of the activities of which we have had such terrible experience in our day in Ireland, in Malaya, in Cyprus and elsewhere. The Romans were always anxious at Passover, when Jerusalem was crowded with strangers. Barabbas seems to have struck a desperate 'blow for freedom'. We know how easily today a cowardly political assassin can be inflated into a national hero. We can see how easily the leaders could persuade the people to ask for the life of the man who had risked his life in the national cause, whereas Jesus had done nothing but talk. Men usually choose the short-cuts to the fulfilment of their desires; the way of Jesus is so long, and seems to offer such scanty dividends in the immediate future. But the choice of Barabbas is always the wrong choice; violence leads to more violence, until there is no end. Every one of the kingdoms and empires of the time of Jesus has long since crumbled into dust; his kingdom, slowly and with many set-backs, has spread irresistibly across the world.

Men are still faced with the choice, Jesus or Barabbas; they are still too easily persuaded, by the hopes of immediate gain, to involve themselves in irreparable loss.

Prayer *O Lord, open our eyes, that on every occasion of choice or decision, we may see the issues in the light of thy truth, and may make our choice according to thy will.* Amen.

Mark 15, vv. 21 to 41

In short unemotional phrases the Evangelist paints for us the central event in human history, the dying of Jesus Christ. There is no description of the grim details of a Roman execution; there is no attempt to stir our emotions by emphasis on the physical sufferings of our Lord. This is just the way it was.

Let us pause to think of the strangeness of it all. Men needed to be saved. God intervened to save them. How would he do it? God is great and all powerful; we might have imagined many ways in which he could have saved us; the one thing that we could never have imagined was this—that he would die for us.

This is a terrible scene; but the most terrible thing about it is that it was brought to pass by people very much like us, part good, part bad, but not on the whole particularly evil—a governor who knew what justice was, but was not quite strong enough to put it into action; religious leaders, who thought that the all-important thing was to safeguard their own position; a crowd that could be too easily swayed by the party-cry of the moment; friends who were taken unaware and lost their heads in the crisis. There is no reason to suppose that, if Jesus came into the world again, the result would be very different today from what it was in AD 29.

This is the condemnation of the world; and yet, strangely, this is the place where the world finds its consolation. The suffering of Jesus in body and mind and spirit was far greater than we can imagine (esp. v. 34); and yet after all he remains master of the situation: to the end his love remains unbroken. It is this that gives us confidence that, in spite of all appearances to the contrary, in this world good is stronger than evil, and love is stronger than hate, and life is stronger than death.

To think over *'Were you there when they crucified my Lord?'*

John 20, vv. 11 to 18 (20, vv. 1 to 23)

The Cross of Jesus was God's great victory over the sin of man. But since to human eyes it appeared as utter defeat, the Resurrection was necessary in order that God's victory might be declared and understood. The Resurrection is a mystery, but it is the foundation of the Church's faith. And this faith is not that somehow, somewhere, the spirit of Jesus survives, but that he conquered death both in body and spirit, and was seen alive of his disciples.

In this first and most beautiful of the Resurrection stories, we may note four points, which are essential and are common to them all:

1. The risen Jesus is manifest only to the eyes of faith. No such vision is given to his enemies; all who see him are already believers.

2. None of those who saw him was expecting the Resurrection; although he had foretold it, it is clear that they had not understood what he said.

3. He was in some way changed, so that those who saw him had difficulty in recognising him.

4. And yet he was the same Jesus; and their fellowship with him after the Resurrection is simply the continuation of the fellowship that they had had with him before his death. It is when he pronounces her name that Mary realises who he is.

In a sense, the whole of the Gospel is contained in these few verses. There is mystery, for the one with whom we have to do is far beyond our power to touch and to hold fast (v. 17). But the whole of Christian faith and Christian life can be summed up as direct and personal fellowship with the risen Christ. Start there, and in time everything else will fall into place.

To think over *'That like as Christ was raised from the dead through the glory of the Father, so we also might walk in newness of life' (Romans 6, v. 4).*

Luke 24, vv. 13 to 35(24, vv. 1 to 49)

In this exquisite story Luke's skill as a narrator reaches perhaps its highest point.

If we compare the accounts of the appearances of the risen Jesus, we shall find that they take place at increasing distances from the tomb, as though to convince the disciples that the risen Jesus can be, and is, present with them wherever they are; when this lesson has been fully learned, the Ascension takes place, and the physical manifestations cease, since the disciples no longer have need of them.

Two special points stand out in this narrative:

1. It was from the Scriptures (i.e. of the Old Testament) that Jesus explained to Cleopas and his companion the meaning of his death. As we shall see in the Acts, after the Resurrection the disciples read the Old Testament with new eyes, and saw in all that had happened to Jesus the fulfilment of a plan of God that had been going forward since the creation of the world.

2. It was in the breaking of the bread that he was known of them. Perhaps these two had often in the past been present when he had broken the bread, and something in his manner of doing it revealed to them who he was. This too has been fulfilled innumerable times in the history of the Church. In the breaking of the bread at the Eucharist more than anywhere else Christians have felt and known that the Risen Christ was with them.

But, once known, he vanishes from their sight. Those who know that he lives have no longer any need of his visible presence. The Resurrection is the secret of faith.

Prayer. *Lord, grant that we who break the Bread and drink of the Cup, may know thee as thou art, and enter into the joy of thy resurrection.   Amen.*

Luke 24, vv. 50 to 53; Matthew 28, vv. 16 to 20

The Ascension of Christ is depicted for us in picture language, and we need not spend too much time trying to interpret the pictures. The disciples had come to believe that Jesus was risen; now it was made plain to them that they must no longer expect such visible fellowship with the Lord as they had enjoyed. It was necessary that his visible presence should be withdrawn, if they were to be free to scatter throughout the world carrying his Gospel.

For at the Ascension the Lord left them three things:

1. A Commission. To preach the Gospel to every creature. If the Church had been faithful to its task, this would long ago have been accomplished. Unhappily, the most evident characteristic of the Church in most ages has been and still is disobedience to its Lord's last command.

2. A Promise. That he would be with them. It was only with the coming of the Holy Spirit that the disciples were able to understand how this promise would be fulfilled. But it has been fulfilled. The presence of Christ has not kept the Church from error and from sin. Parts of the Church have strayed from the faith; parts have sunk into sleep or become moribund; in some areas, e.g. North Africa, the Church has been largely stamped out. But the Church still exists, and the Lord is with it; it has spread across the world, and in our day for the first time is really a world-wide Church.

3. A Hope. The Ascension is the end of the first act of the drama. Now begins the second act, in which the kingdom is invisible, and its cause is committed to the feeble hands of men who have believed in it. But this is not the end—Jesus will come again, and the glory of his kingdom will be finally revealed: it is in this hope that the Church has always lived.

To think over   *If all Churches showed as much enthusiasm for missionary work as that which you attend, what would be the prospects for the evangelization of the world?*

It is extraordinarily hard for us to picture the life of the first Christian groups, when there was no New Testament, no Creed, and no fixed order of worship. These early Christians had three great convictions —that Jesus was the promised Messiah, that he had risen from the dead, and that he was coming again. They had the Scriptures of the Old Testament, and that was about all.

The Gospel spread very rapidly and by the end of the New Testament period Churches were found throughout the Mediterranean world from Mesopotamia to Spain and perhaps beyond. These groups kept in touch with one another through letters and travels and visits of Apostles; but there was room for great diversity among them; and there was always the danger that the Christians would be too much influenced by Jewish ideas, or that they would fall back into pagan ways, or that they would invent for themselves new exaggerations or distortions of the faith. It is this vigorous, adventurous period that is represented for us in the New Testament.

There were four main types of Christian groups:

1. The Aramaic-speaking and generally very conservative Jewish converts.

2. The Jewish converts from 'the Dispersion', who read the Bible in Greek, and were generally more liberal in their outlook.

3. Mixed congregations of Jewish and Gentile converts, such as that at Rome.

4. Churches of purely Gentile origin; these were probably few in the early days.

Each of these groups had different needs and problems, to meet which the various books of the New Testament were written. Much, no doubt, was written that had not survived. The writers did not sit down in their studies to write careful theological treatises (the nearest thing in the New Testament to a treatise is the Epistle to the Hebrews); in the face of some pressing danger they wrote off rapidly urgent and sometimes passionate letters (e.g. Galatians). This is what makes the New Testament so exciting—we can see Christian thought in the very process of growth. It also makes parts of it difficult. Reading parts of St Paul's Epistle is like listening to one end of a telephone conversation: Paul is arguing with somebody and we cannot always hear what the other man is saying. This means that we must read with imagination, and not be too much disturbed if at times the full meaning escapes us.

By the end of the first century the great creative period had come to an end. In outline all the truth about Jesus Christ had been worked out. The Churches were beginning to settle down. The New Testament as we know it was beginning to take shape. For a period some other books such as the Epistle of Barnabas were included in the New Testament of some Churches; and some of the books which we now use, such as Hebrews and Revelation, were not used in certain areas. By AD 140 the New Testament, almost exactly as we have it, was in use throughout the Church; since then the Church has added nothing to it, and to the New Testament the Church has always gone back for the renewal of its life.

Of very few books in the New Testament can we say exactly where and by whom and when they were written. The following tentative summary (omitting the Gospels, which we have already dealt with) may be found helpful by some readers:

49–56: Earlier Epistles of St Paul: *1* and *2 Thessalonians, Galatians, 1* and *2 Corinthians, Romans.*

56–64: Later Epistles of St Paul: *Colossians, Philemon, Philippians, Ephesians.*

About the same time or rather later: *James, 1 Peter, Hebrews.*

80–90: *Acts of the Apostles.*

90–100: *Epistles of John, Revelation.*

The *Epistles to Timothy* and *Titus, 2 Peter* and *John* are thought by many scholars to be the latest books in the New Testament Canon.

WORKING IT OUT

☐ The Acts of the Apostles might be called 'From Jerusalem to Rome'. It is not a complete history of the Early Church; in a series of very carefully chosen incidents, it shows how the faith spread from Jerusalem, the centre of the Jewish faith, to Rome, the capital of the Roman Empire. Its contents can be summarised under five heads:

1. Beginnings of Christian theology, seen in the speeches of Peter and the other leaders.

2. Beginnings of Christian organisation—apostles, elders and so on.

3. Dangers to the Church from outer persecution and inner perversion.

4. The grave threat of division in the Church and the way in which it was treated.

5. The generally friendly, if not favourable, attitude of the Roman powers towards the Christian Church.

Acts was written later than most of the Epistles; but we take it first because it gives the necessary background of history into which we can fit the Epistles. It does not tell us all that we would like to know: but without it how much would we know of the most creative period in the history of the Church?

Acts 2, vv. 1 to 21

It is difficult to know exactly what happened on the day of Pentecost. Most readers concentrate on the outward signs—the wind, the fire, etc. But these are not very important, and there are many parallels to such experiences in times of great religious excitement. The old interpretation was that the Apostles were given the gift of speaking languages which they had never learned; we now see it to be more probable that this was some form of ecstatic speech which was beyond the control of those who spoke. These were all passing phenomena; what we have to ask is—What were the permanent results of what the apostles recognised as the coming of the Spirit whom Jesus had promised?

1. First is the transformation of the Christian fellowship; these very ordinary men were lifted out of themselves into a new fellowship in which they thought and felt and experienced as one man.

2. Second is the beginning of the Christian witness. Since the Resurrection they had said nothing to any man. Now they begin to proclaim the Resurrection from the housetops, though they know that they do so at the risk of their lives. What was important was not that they 'spoke with tongues' but that they set forth 'the mighty works of God' (v. 11).

3. The contagion of the new fellowship. As soon as the excitement had died down a little and Peter was able to express himself in intelligible speech, many of the crowd felt themselves irresistibly drawn towards and into this experience of which they had been the witnesses.

It is on these things that the Christian Church has depended ever since Pentecost—the power of a supernatural fellowship, the witness of quite ordinary people to Jesus Christ, the contagion of Christian affection. That is why Pentecost is called the birthday of the Church. Because all these things are so lacking today, our Churches are not very much like Churches of Jesus Christ.

To think over *Try to describe in modern terms what it would be like if Pentecost came to your Church today.*

Acts 2, vv. 22 to 36 (2, vv. 22 to 47)

Great interest attaches to their first proclamation of the Christian message. Evidently this is a summary of a much longer speech; but the author of Acts must have been working either from the recollections of those who heard it, or an earlier written account, and the points stand out quite clearly.

1. The central issue is the Resurrection—the new thing which the Christians had to declare. A great Indian bishop was once asked where we should start in proclaiming the Gospel to those who have never heard it. His answer was 'You must start with the Resurrection'. This may seem surprising, but after all it makes sense; what matters is not that someone named Jesus lived a long time ago, but that there is a living Saviour who is available to us today.

2. The hearers were Jews, and therefore it was necessary to link up the message of Jesus Christ with the witness of the Old Testament. It seemed paradoxical and incredible that the Messiah should have been betrayed and killed. But more and more the Christians came to see that what at first sight was so strange was in line with an age-long purpose of God, of which hints and foreshadowings were given in the Old Testament.

3. There was a practical step to be taken by those who believed the message—they must be baptised. John the Baptist had baptised in preparation of a Kingdom that was yet to come; the Christians from the start baptised 'into Jesus Christ', that is into the fellowship of his death and resurrection, by which the Kingdom had been brought in. But this included, of course, the joyful hope of that manifestation of the Kingdom that is yet to come. If we have been baptised, that is the meaning of our baptism.

Prayer *O Lord, grant us so perfectly, and without all doubt, to believe in thy Son Jesus Christ, that our faith in thy sight may never be reproved.*   Amen.

Acts 8, vv. 26 to 40

Much of the Acts is taken up with sermons and public ministry. Today's reading gives us a fascinating glimpse of the Christian Evangelist engaged in personal witness to an individual. This helps us to realise the quiet and unobtrusive way in which the Gospel spread through the whole Mediterranean world. Four points may be noted as typical.

1. A prepared spirit. The Ethiopian nobleman was presumably a Gentile; but, as he had been up to Jerusalem to worship, it is clear that he had been attracted by the Jewish faith, and was a seeker after God.

2. The Old Testament approach. The nobleman was reading Isaiah 53; this was a passage which must have been very often used by Christian preachers to lead the minds of their hearers on from the Old Testament to an understanding of the meaning of the death of Jesus Christ.

3. The direct challenge to faith in Jesus Christ. 'He preached unto him Jesus.' This is a note which is all too often missing from modern preaching.

4. Baptism immediately, and after much less preparation than would be thought necessary for converts in the mission field today. For the nobleman it was a case of now or never; and presumably Philip relied upon the power of the Holy Spirit to keep him steadfast in his faith in his distant home.

This is the kind of thing which is constantly happening today in railway trains and aeroplanes and other unexpected places. Naturally such quiet Christian witness does not hit the head-lines; it may be even more important in the life of the Church than many more public ministries.

To think over   *Are you prepared for the same kind of thing to happen to you as happened to Philip?*

Acts 9, vv. 1 to 22 (9, vv. 1 to 31)

The conversion of Saul of Tarsus, the bitter enemy of the Christian faith, is often taken as the typical example of a 'sudden conversion'. But it may well be doubted whether there is really any such thing; the decisive experience may come in a moment, but there seems always to be a long period of preparation. Saul had been jealous for the Law of God. His persecution of the Christians had been the expression of a real loyalty, though as he afterwards recognised a mistaken loyalty, to what he believed to be the truth. (The people it is hardest to convert are those who are indifferent to everything.) He had stood by at the martyrdom of Stephen (Acts 7:58 and 8:1), and had seen how a Christian could die.

We are unlikely to undergo such an experience as that of Saul of Tarsus, but there are three elements in his conversion which are of universal relevance:

1. Every genuine Christian conversion is a meeting with the Risen Jesus. Sometimes, but not always, this is accompanied by an acute sense of sinfulness.

2. The central factor in conversion is not emotion (usually the less emotion the better!) but obedience:' Lord what will you have me do?'

3. The immediate demand of the Lord may be something of extreme simplicity: 'Arise, and go into the city'. Innumerable Christians could give a similar record of their experience, when they met the Living Christ; what he said to them may have been something as simple as 'Go and tell X that you are sorry' for some wrong that has been done. Obedience in what seems a very small thing may be the real point of turning from the self-centred to the Christ-centred life.

Prayer *Lord, if we are unconverted, convert us; if we are converted, strengthen us; and whether we be converted or unconverted, teach us the joy of ready and immediate obedience to thy will.* Amen.

Acts 17, vv. 16 to 34 (17, vv. 1 to 34)

This is our only specimen in Acts of a sermon preached to an unprepared Gentile audience. Athens had fallen a good deal from the eminence of her classical days, but was still one of the intellectual capitals of the ancient world; and St Paul may well have felt somewhat embarrassed as he stood on Areopagus to preach to this collection of Greek philosophers with their acute and critical minds.

Certainly this address is very different from his other sermons in Acts and from the Epistles. But it is important not to exaggerate the extent to which he adapts his message to his Greek audience. Like any good preacher he makes contact with his hearers through a local allusion—to the shrine of an Unknown God; and he quotes a tag from the not very good Greek poet Aratus. But the two essential points of his message—creation and resurrection—would be wholly strange to his hearers. For the Greeks, with all their wisdom, had not grasped the principle so sublimely set forth in the first verse of the Bible, that God created the universe and is therefore the sovereign Lord of it. And the idea that a dead man could rise again to be the judge of all men was so strange an idea as to be met with incredulous laughter.

It is remarkable, however, that in the whole speech there is no mention of the Cross; and it is impressive that, writing to the Corinthians, the people of the city to which Paul moved on after completing his mission at Athens, he wrote: 'I determined not to know anything among you, save Jesus Christ, and him crucified' (1 Cor. 2:2). The Cross and the Resurrection are in fact inseparable; and Paul never again seems to have made the mistake of trying to separate them.

To think over   *How far can a missionary rightly go in trying to adapt his message to the outlook of his hearers?*

Acts 28, vv. 16 to 31 (28, vv. 1 to 31)

Rome was by far the most important city in the ancient world, even more important than London is in the British Commonwealth. It had always been Paul's aim to visit it, and now his aim is realised. But not as he had imagined; he comes as a captive, he is to spend the rest of his life in more or less rigorous captivity, and finally is to die as a martyr.

Note first that Paul did not found the Church in Rome; there were already brethren there. So it often was in those days. Christians on their travels took the Gospel with them; won converts and brought Churches into existence. The Apostles arrived later to organise the Churches and to appoint elders (Acts 14:23). The three greatest Churches of the ancient world were Antioch, Alexandria, and Rome; of not one of them can we say exactly by whom it was founded. So it ought to be today.

Further, note that here in Rome also Paul turns first to the Jews. In spite of many disappointments and persecutions, he sticks to his principle 'To the Jew first, and also to the Greek'. If only the Jews can be converted, they will be the natural missionaries to all the world.

In later times, when the Empire persecuted the Christians, there was a tendency to regard the Empire as the great enemy; but at the time of Paul's arrival in Rome this change had not yet taken place. The Roman Empire had given peace and unity to the world from Hadrian's wall to the Euphrates; and Paul regarded this as providentially ordered, as a means to make possible the rapid spread of the Gospel. The rulers are still servants of God in their order and function, and it is the Jews who put hindrances in the way of the Gospel. So, though Paul is a prisoner of the Romans, the last verse of this very carefully written book gives a picture of him still free to bear witness in Rome, and the very last word (in Greek as in English) is 'no man hindering him'.

Prayer *O Lord, give such peace to the nations of the world, that, through the faithful preaching of thy Gospel, they may become the kingdoms of thy Son our Lord.*   Amen.

THINKING IT THROUGH

☐ The reading of Acts has given us the framework of the expansion of the Christian Church in the generation after the death of Jesus; now we must take a look at the internal developments of that time. It was a period of intense intellectual activity; within fifty years the teachers of the Church had worked out all the main types of interpretation of the work of Christ, and since that time the Church has never had to go outside the limits they laid down, though it has constantly discovered fresh aspects of the truth in their writings and teachings.

The greatest part of this work was done by St Paul. His was a life of intense labour, intense suffering (see 2 Cor. 11:24–30) and intense thought. In his surviving epistles, which can easily be read through in four hours, he has dealt with almost every part of Christian truth and Christian practice. It would be absurd to attempt to summarise his teaching in a page; but the reader may find it convenient to have three sign posts to guide him, as he tackles the readings from a writer who is always difficult to follow just because of the concentration of his thought.

Paul has shown us:

1. *The meaning of salvation.* Sinful man can deserve nothing and can earn nothing. Salvation can come to him only as the free gift of God, and this gift is seen and offered in the dying of Jesus for our sins. This is the safeguard against the perpetual tendency to turn the Gospel into a new law, by the keeping of which we can earn salvation.

2. *The meaning of the Spirit.* Through the Spirit, who is the Spirit of liberty, Jesus is always at work among those who believe in him. This means that we must always turn afresh to him for new light and new guidance in the problems by which we are faced. This is the safeguard against the imprisonment of the Gospel in the past.

3. *The meaning of the Church.* Paul had much to do with the great controversy in which the free entry of the Gentiles into the Church was secured. But his doctrine of the Church is more than this; it shows that God's purpose in the world is to be fulfilled in a people, a company, a fellowship, in which all nations are to be gathered into the Body of Christ. This is the safeguard against the individualism which imagines that religion is just what happens between God and my own soul.

1 Corinthians 1, vv. 18 to 2, v. 5

Christianity is not a religion of ideas; it is the proclamation of things that have happened, of things that God has done. There is much interest at present in the ancient religions of the East, and people will often tell you that there are very good ideas in Buddhism and Vedanta and so on. No doubt there are. But does any of these religions tell you that God thought it would be a good idea to suffer and die for our sins?

If that is true all men's usual ideas about God are made to stand on their heads. The Jew thinks of God as power, and the Greeks think of him as wisdom. Whoever could imagine that God's power could be seen in the utter weakness of a man dying on a Cross, or that his wisdom could be seen in the utter failure of what might have been a promising career? But Paul is bold to affirm that Christ *is* the power and the wisdom of God, and that it is in his Cross that we have the assurance that this is so (v. 24).

In the days of St Paul this preaching was a terrible scandal to both Jews and Greeks. It is still a terrible scandal to the humanists and the scientists and the communists and the Brahmans—to everyone in fact who thinks conventionally in terms of wisdom and power. Inevitably the Gospel is a scandal to ordinary men—why should our salvation depend on a crucified Jew? But that is what the Gospel is about, and we must not try to make it mean anything else. That is why a miracle is always needed, to enable men to see that Jesus really is the power and the wisdom of God.

To think over *'The Gospel is the thing men most love to hear.' 'The Gospel is the thing men most hate to hear.'*

1 Corinthians 12, vv. 4 to 14 and vv. 26 to 31 (12, vv. 1 to 31)

We have already remarked that the Holy Spirit is central in the teaching of St Paul. But much had to be done to make the teaching clear. As on the day of Pentecost, the coming of the Spirit was sometimes accompanied by great excitement, and the strange phenomenon of 'speaking in tongues'. The carryings-on of the 'Spirit-possessed' seem to have caused much disturbance in the worship of the Corinthian Christians.

St Paul does not deny the existence of such phenomena, or their relation to the gift of the Spirit; he does deny that they are specially important, and recognises that they may be dangerous, as making those who have received them arrogant.

1. The Spirit is the Spirit of Christ; since we are all in Christ, we have all received a share of the Spirit. To be a Christian is to be one who has received the Spirit.

2. The Spirit is not given as a kind of prize to the individual, but for the service of the community.

3. The Spirit is the Spirit of unity; and this can be realised only as all Christians contribute their special gifts to the well-being of the whole, just as the separate parts of the body work together in unity.

4. This means that not only the conspicuous gifts, such as preaching and prophesying, but also the more humble gifts of service and administration must be recognised as gifts of the Spirit (v. 28ff).

The Spirit does not turn us all out in one pattern, as though Christians were all of a type. He is the Spirit of liberty, and sets us free to be truly ourselves. Since God has created us all different, the Spirit makes us even more different from one another than we were before, and by these differences the Church is enriched. This is really obvious. The preacher who is content just to be himself is always interesting to listen to; the preacher who conforms to a type, however eloquent, soon becomes dreadfully boring.

Prayer *O Lord Jesus Christ, help us to use the good gifts of thy Spirit not for ourselves but for the building up of thy Body in love.*   Amen.

1 Corinthians 13, vv. 1 to 13

This chapter is universally recognised as one of the supreme treasures of Christian literature. St Paul has been arguing against those who attached too much importance to the exciting and ecstatic phenomena of Spirit-possession; now he lifts the argument to a wholly different plane. How do we know whether people have received the Holy Spirit or not? Simply by observing whether they have become more loving or not. If they are hard and unloving, it does not matter whether they speak in a hundred tongues or do miracles—it is not the Holy Spirit of the loving Jesus that is at work in them.

There is a false love as well as the true. The love of many parents for their children is possessive. Where this is the case, the parents are really loving themselves, and their love imprisons and weakens their children. In true love there is always an element of self-sacrifice, even in the love of God. Such love is patient, humble, gentle; seeks nothing for itself; desires only that the other should be exalted. Only so can it be kept pure and free from taint.

Of all material things the principle laid down in *Alice in Wonderland* is true; 'That means that the more there is of mine the less there is of yours'. With love it is not so; the more there is of mine, the more there is for everybody. Love generates love, and is reflected back in love; and the blessedness of the heavenly Kingdom is just the never-ending increase of love.

We *believe* in that which we do not see. When we see Jesus face to face, faith will be lost in sight. We *hope* for that which is yet to come: when all is accomplished, hope will be swallowed up in accomplishment. But love remains for ever, and can only increase. St Paul is in full agreement with the truth we shall meet later in St John, that 'God is Love', and 'Love is of God'.

To think over   *'O Lord, who hast taught us that all our doings without charity are nothing worth.' Why?*

1 Corinthians 15, vv. 1 to 17 and vv. 50 to 58 (15, vv. 1 to 58)

This is one of the few points at which the Epistles make direct contact with the Gospels. Critics of the Christian faith sometimes draw attention to the long gap between the dates at which things happen and the dates at which they are written down. But is the gap so very long? This Epistle was written less than thirty years after the death of Christ; and those of us who are getting older know well how clearly we can remember the events of thirty years ago. But many scholars think that Paul is here quoting an even earlier formula, which the Corinthians knew, because it formed part of the instruction they had received before their baptism. If so, this brings us very near indeed to the date of the actual happenings.

Paul is arguing from the Resurrection of Christ to our own destiny. Christianity does not teach the natural immortality of the soul— that is a Greek idea. It does teach that God can as well raise us up as he raised Christ from the dead. This is the meaning of the resurrection of the body—not that our physical bodies will be resuscitated, but that we shall be raised as complete persons, such as the experiences of life and faith in Christ have made us, capable of personal fellowship with God and with one another, in the glory of the eternal Kingdom. This will mean an astonishing transformation, such as now we cannot even imagine—but the Resurrection of Christ is an indication of the change that God is able to bring about in us also.

The last verse shows us the true meaning of Christian 'otherworldliness'. If we have the eternal perspective, we can come back to be patient, humble, and indomitable in our daily work, and to glorify God in every single thing that is given us to do.

For further work *Compare 1 Corinthians 15 with the Gospel narratives of the Resurrection, noting similarities and differences.*

2 Corinthians 5, vv. 11 to 21 (5, vv. 1 to 21)

In 2 Corinthians Paul shows us more of his own heart than in any other letter; it is a tender, eloquent and moving document. Here he speaks to us of:

1. The Christian's commission—an ambassador for Christ intreating men on God's behalf (v. 20). We ought to be pleading with God for mercy on our sins; instead God is pleading with us to be good enough to allow ourselves to be saved. How ridiculous! But that is the measure of the hardness of our hearts.

2. The Christian's motive—'The love of Christ constraineth us' (v. 14). If a man knows Christ, you do not need to tell him to pass the message on—you cannot keep him quiet! If a man knows what it is to be loved by Christ, it becomes intolerable to him that others should go on living and dying without the knowledge of that love.

3. The Christian's message—'Him who knew no sin he made to be sin on our behalf' (v. 21). How can we ever grasp it? Fr Damien went to work among the lepers in Molokai, and after some years he was a leper himself. It is something like that. Christ came and lived among us and caught our disease and died of it—and his death is our cure. We can see what that means practically. We cannot fall so low, but Christ will come down as low as we are to lift us up. We cannot run away so far, but Christ will be after us. We cannot hide ourselves away so deep, but Christ will find us out. And then all things will become new.

It all seems very absurd. But it happens to be true.

Prayer   *Lord, give us grace never to stop being surprised at thy Gospel.*   Amen.

Romans 6, vv. 1 to 14 (6, vv. 1 to 23)

What is the relationship between faith and baptism? In the early Church the question did not arise. It was taken for granted that anyone who believed would as soon as possible be baptised (like St Paul himself: see Acts 22:16). In time of persecution it was unlikely that anyone would offer himself for baptism, unless he had a real and living faith.

Paul is thinking in terms of the baptism of adults by immersion, as it is still practised in many mission fields. Here the complete disappearance of the candidate under the water is very like a real burial, and his emergence is very like a real resurrection (v. 4). Nothing could more dramatically set forth the revolutionary character of faith in Christ as a complete separation from the past, and the adoption of a completely new principle of life. This is less dramatic, but no less real, in the case of those who have been born in Christian families. For the principle of the old life in all of us is self—self-pleasing, self-expression, self-realisation; and this self has utterly to die and to be replaced by the new principle of life in Christ, if we are to 'walk in newness of life' (v. 4). The old self is singularly unwilling to die.

This is what is sacramentally effected for us in baptism; but it has to become a living experience of faith. This comes about not by any effort of our own will, but simply through recognition of what God has done *for* us in the historic events of Christ's death and resurrection; and the belief that God can do the same *in* us through the Holy Spirit, who makes present and real to us the whole work and victory of Christ.

Prayer *O merciful God, grant that the old Adam in this child may be so buried, that the new man may be raised up in him.* Amen. (Service of Holy Baptism)

Romans 8, vv. 18 to 39 (8, vv. 1 to 39)

Romans, chapters 5 to 8 is a series of rising climaxes on the Christian life—free from wrath (5), free from sin (6), free from the law (7), free from death (8).

Paul had suffered more than almost any other man, and his enemies seem to have adduced these sufferings as evidence that God could not be on his side—a subject on which the apostle appears to have been very sensitive. In this passage he surveys the whole problem of suffering in a new light, and has written the profoundest passage on suffering in the whole Bible. Suffering may be merely destructive, but it can also be creative, a part of that creative suffering through which new life comes into being. All suffering—of Christ, who brought in the new age, of Christians who are persecuted for his sake, the ordinary sufferings that are part of the daily life of men, the dumb suffering of the animals (for many the hardest problem of all)—can be seen as birth-pangs, the striving through which, amid the old creation, God is bringing the new into being. If this is true, salvation takes on a far more splendid perspective than we usually allow it: salvation of the individual; salvation of the Church; salvation of the human race; salvation of the whole creation, delivered from the futility and frustration and imperfection to which it is subject, and delivered into the perfection that God has in store for it. What that would mean we cannot imagine; Paul just lifts the curtain for a moment and lets it drop again.

But he has given us enough to live by, even if it falls to our lot to suffer. Christ has suffered for us; he is with us in our sufferings, or rather it is he who suffers in us. Therefore we need not be afraid, since nothing can separate us from the indestructible love of God given to us in him.

To think over   *Does St Paul's doctrine seem to you to make sense of the problem and mystery of suffering?*

Philippians 2, vv. 1 to 11 (2, vv. 1 to 18)

Philippians is one of the latest of Paul's Epistles, written when he was already a prisoner in Rome; yet no other Epistle is so filled with the spirit of quiet joy.

Today's reading is a good example of Paul's method; he cannot deal with the simplest practical problem without calling up the heaviest theological artillery. Apparently the Philippian Christians were not getting on too well with one another (see also 4:2–3). Paul does not give them good advice—he writes them a tremendous passage about the mind that was in Christ, when he took upon him the form of a servant, and that ought to be in all of us.

Some scholars think that Paul is here (vv. 6–11) quoting an early Christian hymn. This is possible; but we have seen already enough of Paul's poetic power to know that he may well have written these verses himself. The key word is 'Wherefore' (v. 9). We would perhaps have written 'The Jews crucified Jesus, *but* God raised him up and gave him glory'. Paul does not think so much in terms of *contrast* between suffering and glory. Because God is such as he is, the glory is the inevitable *consequence* of the humiliation and suffering. This is one of the passages in which Paul speaks most clearly about the *pre-existence* of Christ. All Christians believed that he was alive after his death. It was only later that they asked the question as to his being before his human birth, and only gradually that they came to realise that it was the eternal Son of God who came into the world for our sakes. This is the marvel which, if we stop to think about it seriously, must leave us speechless with astonishment and gratitude.

To think over   *A distinguished preacher said: 'Most people will tell you that the way up is up, I want to tell you that the way up is down.'*

The Epistle to Philemon

St Paul must have written hundreds of short personal letters: we may well be thankful that chance, or providence, has preserved for us this one exquisite specimen.

We know nothing of the circumstances except what can be gathered from the letter itself. Onesimus, the slave of Philemon, an eminent member of the Church of Colossae, had run away from his master, and like most of the rest of the riff-raff of that time had drifted to Rome. There he had somehow come into contact with Paul and been converted. The question arose as to what must happen next. Paul's handling of the situation is a marvellous specimen of common sense and Christian courtesy.

1. Onesimus must go back. We can well imagine his reluctance to do so—there was almost no limit to the cruelty with which a master could treat a runaway slave. But the acceptance of Christ as Lord does not set him free from his duties to his earthly master. *2.* Paul does not say that slavery is wrong. He must have hoped that it would disappear; but this could come about only through a profound influence of Christ on society. *3.* Masters as well as slaves have duties. Paul does not say that Philemon is to set Onesimus free; he does say that for the future he is to treat him as a brother. *4.* The apostle does not try to exercise authority or to issue orders; with beautiful humility he puts himself in the position of a petitioner. *5.* He undertakes himself to compensate Philemon for the financial loss that he has suffered through the absence of his slave.

We do not know how the story ended; but the fact that the letter has survived suggests that it ended happily. How did Paul learn to deal with such a problem? Surely from the way in which God in Christ had treated him.

A little practice   *Try your hand at writing a Pauline epistle on behalf of a boy or girl who has run away from school.*

Ephesians 3, vv. 1 to 21

Most of Paul's letters are highly personal. Ephesians is by contrast impersonal; and many scholars think that it may have been written not by Paul himself, but by one of his disciples as a summary of the master's teaching. There is also evidence that it was written not to one Church, but as a circular to many of the Churches of Asia Minor.

The main subject of the letter is unity—God's purpose to bring back all things to unity in Christ. In this passage Paul is thinking specially of the age-long division between Jews and Gentiles, and the way in which this has been done away in Christ. All that God now asks is faith in Jesus Christ: the same demand is made of both Jews and Gentiles; there can now no more be any question of privilege or inferiority, since all enter together into one fellowship on the same terms.

Contemplation of this great mystery lifts Paul up into the wonderful prayer with which the chapter ends (vv. 14–21). This is, in fact, a great statement of the whole meaning of the Christian faith. Every word deserves careful study. Here we find—power; the Spirit; the indwelling Christ; stability; fellowship with all other Christians; increase in knowledge and in love; the centrality of the love of Christ; triumphant fulfilment; praise and adoration of God. A study of this prayer will convict us of the poverty of the prayers that we offer for ourselves and for other people, and will open out before us a new idea of what prayer really is.

For further study   *Look up and compare Paul's prayers for his friends in Philippians 1, vv. 9 to 11 ; Colossians 1, vv. 9 to 12.*

Ephesians 4, vv. 1 to 16 (4, vv. 1 to 32)

As in other Epistles the great climax of doctrinal instruction is immediately followed by practical teaching about the Christian life.

It is God's will to 'sum up all things in Christ' (1:10), to bring them back to that unity which he has planned for them. That has not yet been brought about. But in the Church, the Body of Christ, that unity has already been given and revealed; division has been done away, through one faith in one God, and one baptism into one Christ. But this unity, though given by God, is not something that can simply be taken for granted. It has to be maintained (*'being enthusiastic* to maintain the unity,' says the Greek). We have to press forward to yet fuller unity (v. 13).

St Paul knew by experience how difficult it was to maintain the unity. It was constantly threatened—by personal rivalries and loyalties, by exaggerated emphases, by false teachers. Through the whole of Church history we recognise the same problem. Today the first thing an outside observer would notice about the Church is not its unity. In almost every parish there are divisions caused by pride, gossip and backbiting. In the Church of England there are sects and parties which, instead of being content just to challenge one another to deeper devotion to Christ, waste their time and the strength of the Church in fruitless argument. We speak of 'the Church'; but what we see is 'the Churches'—the Church of Rome, the Church of England, the Reformed Churches, and so on.

One of the great movements in the world today is that for the renewal of the visible unity of Christ's Church. To this we should all be committed—both to working for the unity of Christians where we are, and to praying for the unity of all the scattered people of God.

Prayer *Regard not our sins, but the faith of thy Church, and grant unto it that peace and unity which are agreeable to thy will.* Amen.

LATER BOOKS OF THE NEW TESTAMENT

☐ The two most surprising things about the New Testament are its unity and its variety. It is all about Jesus Christ; but each writer exercises an extraordinary liberty and originality in depicting and interpreting Jesus Christ for us.

We now turn to four short books, each of which is wonderfully different from the others. Each deals with the problem of faith; each is written in a situation where the true faith is being threatened.

James is the most Jewish book in the New Testament; Jesus is mentioned in it only twice. Here the problem is that of a conventional faith and its consequences in a low moral standard. Faith has to be awakened to understand its consequences in action.

Hebrews is the work of a brilliant anonymous author, whose Greek is better than that of any other New Testament writer. Here the danger is that of apostasy, falling away from the faith. Faith to this writer is a forward-looking faith, which moves steadily onwards to the fulfilment of the promises of God.

1 Peter is believed by many scholars to have been originally a sermon preached to converts at their baptism, perhaps by St Peter, perhaps by someone else using the teaching that Peter was wont to give. Here faith is threatened by persecution. Faith means standing fast in face of hardship and suffering.

1 John is written to those whose faith is in danger of being corrupted by false teachers, who claim a higher knowledge but deny the reality of the Gospel. Faith must go back to Jesus, really manifest for us in the flesh.

Finally, to complete our study, we come back to two of the latest New Testament books, at which we have already taken a glance. Most of the Bible deals with history; but, as these two books make clear, all history must be seen in the light of eternity.

The Gospel of John is the picture of the eternal Word of God, who really entered into time, and lived among us, and so brought to us the gift of eternal life.

The Revelation lifts our eyes above the tragedies and disasters of this life to the triumph of God; to the eternal city, and to the fulness and completion of our own redemption.

James 2, vv. 14 to 26 (2, vv. 1 to 26)

Paul says that faith without works is enough (Galatians 2:16); James says that faith and works are both necessary. A great deal has been made of this apparent contradiction. But in reality the two writers are talking about exactly the same thing—total commitment of ourselves to Jesus Christ. Paul says, 'You do not have to make yourself good, before you trust in Christ—you can come as a sinner, because God loves sinners.' James say, 'If you go on without a complete change in your manner of living, it shows that you have not really committed yourself to Christ at all.' True faith is a narrow way. With too much emphasis on Paul's point of view there is the pitfall of antinomianism: 'If your belief is correct, it doesn't matter what you do.' With too much of James there is the pitfall of legalism: 'As long as a man's actions are right, it doesn't much matter what he believes.' A good admixture of Paul and James will keep us in the right way.

The word 'works' is being used by the two writers in two quite different senses. Paul is saying, 'Nothing that a man can do can commend him to God or atone for sin;

> Could my zeal no respite know,
> Could my tears for ever flow,
> All for sin would not atone;
> Thou must save and thou alone.'

James is saying, 'Good works are not what you do in order to be accepted by God; they are what you cannot help doing, if you have been accepted by God.' Paul would entirely agree; after all, a great part of his epistles is taken up with telling us how we are to live in order to show our love and gratitude to God who has redeemed us in Jesus Christ. This is the service of free men.

To think over *Which of the two pitfalls mentioned above is the more dangerous, and which is more prevalent in the Churches today?*

Hebrews 2, vv. 1 to 17 (1, v.1 to 2, v. 17)

The Epistle to the Hebrews has three special characteristics:

1. Emphasis on the present glory of Christ. He is the great High Priest, who has entered for us into the heavenly sanctuary, as the high priest under the old law entered once a year into the most holy place in the Temple.

2. Imaginative interpretation of the Old Testament. In Psalm 8 (quoted here vv. 6–7), the Psalmist is speaking of mankind in general. But, says the writer, this wonderful destiny was not fulfilled in mankind as a whole; it was fulfilled only in Christ—fulfilled in him, however, only in order that it might in due course be fulfilled in all men.

3. But this can come about only if Christ is fully and really part of the human race; hence the third special emphasis on the manhood of Christ, in the reality of his human experience and of his suffering (see also 4:14–16 and 5:7–10). The Epistles very rarely quote actual words of Jesus, but we can find countless points of correspondence between Epistles and Gospels, and can see how the teaching of Jesus had penetrated the life of the Church, even before it came to be written down. Jesus had said that those who do the will of God are his sisters and his brethren (Mark 3:33–35). Our writer has taken up the same word, 'he is not ashamed to call them brethren' (v. 11), and has given the word an even wider application than it had in the life of Jesus himself.

To think over   *The word 'Brother' is not often used by Christians in speaking of Jesus or in addressing him. Would it be a good thing if the term came back into more general use?*

Hebrews 11, vv. 17 to 40 (11, vv. 1 to 40)

The readers of this Epistle were in danger of clinging to the old ways, instead of going forward boldly to face an unknown future, as the writer felt that they ought to do. To encourage them he draws up this wonderful roll of honour of the heroes of the faith.

In this Epistle, 'faith' constantly means just that—going forward, trusting simply in God and in his promises, to enter an unknown land and to face an unknown future—like Abraham who went out not knowing whither he went (v. 8). The whole can be summed up in the phrase, 'he endured, as seeing him who is invisible.'

The first Christians had to go forward in the faith that their new message could become the basis of a world-wide religion. It was incredible, and it has taken a very long time to happen. But in our day for the first time Christianity is a world-wide religion.

A hundred and fifty years ago, missionaries had to believe that a way would be opened up into the closed lands of India, China and Japan. Their faith was honoured and the existence of 'the younger Churches' is a reward of that faith.

Today we have to believe that the Church will stand and make headway against communism, against our terrible western secularism, and against the revival of the ancient religions of the East. It is hard to believe. But only those who see the invisible and believe the incredible are able to do great exploits in the Name of Christ.

Prayer *O thou sole source of peace and righteousness, take now the veil from every heart, and join us in one communion with thy prophets and saints who have trusted in thee and were not ashamed.* Amen.

1 Peter 1, vv. 1 to 12 (1, vv. 1 to 25)

There is no doubt that it was the exuberant joy of the early Christians that made them such effective witnesses for Christ (v. 8). There was not much joy in the world in which they lived. The Roman Empire had made life safer for most people than it had ever been before, but it had also made it rather dull. Art had become imitative. Both Greek and Latin literature had come to the end of their greatest creative periods. A quiet melancholy suffused a great deal of life, rising, as time went on and the barbarian invasions became a serious menace, into acute anxiety. In this society, the Christians stood out as the really happy people—as those who knew what they were there for, and where they were going and what they had to do. Is there not a close parallel here with our own day? But are Christians today recognisable as the specially joyful people?

What was the source of early Christian joy? It was the Resurrection (v. 3) and nothing else. Will a man live again after he has died? Philosophy could give only a doubtful answer, and modern philosophy has not added much to what Plato wrote more than 2,000 years ago. The mystery religions held out hope of a blessed immortality after death, but they could give no rational reason for their belief. Even the Old Testament failed to give a perfectly clear answer. And now the question was answered. Jesus has risen, and so we know. In one sense we are still waiting for our inheritance—we are not yet there (v. 4); in another sense we already have it, because of the assurance that Jesus gives (v. 9), and in that we rejoice.

To think over *'The real difference is that some men believe in the resurrection of Jesus Christ and others do not.' Do you agree?*

1 Peter 4, vv. 7 to 19 (4, vv. 1 to 19)

When this passage was written, Christians were still inclined to regard persecution as 'a strange thing'. This means that probably the central part of 1 Peter dates from AD 63–4, the period when Nero was launching persecution on Christians in Rome. From the beginning Christians had been used to tumults and attack by the mob, often stimulated by the envy of the Jews; but on the whole the Roman power had not been unfavourable to them and had kept the peace. Now it seemed indeed strange that the protector had turned to be the persecutor.

The apostle's advice to Christians in time of persecution is very plain and simple. Maintain courtesy in relations with all people. Avoid every occasion of just punishment. Bear your testimony gently but firmly. But above all it is from the example of the Redeemer that his teaching is drawn. 'The Spirit of glory and the Spirit of God resteth upon you.' Glory is not simply something that follows upon suffering; there is a glory in suffering itself, borne in the Name of Christ, and borne as he bore it. It is there that the splendour of God most evidently appears.

It has always seemed strange to Christians that they should be persecuted—they are such innocent and harmless people whose only desire is to do others good. And yet persecution is really natural. Christians are very dangerous people, since the Gospel constitutes a threat to the very heart of every non-Christian system of thought, and to every existing order of society. Even in our own comparatively Christianised society, if you take the line of uncompromising loyalty to Christ, you may quickly find yourself in opposition to your dearest friends, to the general opinion of society, and perhaps even to the laws of your country. Then you will find that the teeth of persecution are just as sharp today as they were in 63–4.

To think over *The Church exists only because in every generation there have been enough men and women who were willing, if necessary, to die for Christ. Are you one of them?*

1 John 1, v. 1 to 2, v. 6

The Bible is mostly about things that God has *done*—he made the world, he sent his Son, etc. But, in order to meet the menace of false teaching, St John has to go behind this, and ask the question, Who *is* God? No man can ever finally answer this question, but St John gives us a number of wonderful pictures, of which the first is *God is Light* (v. 5).

This means that God is 'all of a piece', without any contradiction. He is always the same. Where we cannot see his work or his methods (e.g. What does he do with and for those who have never had a chance to hear of Jesus Christ?), we can be certain that he is just such a God as we have known in Jesus Christ. When his way of handling us is perplexing, we can be certain that all his purposes are good.

What he asks from us is utter sincerity (walking in the light v. 7) to match his own—to accept the truth about ourselves, not to pretend to be better than we are, not to be afraid of reality. (And then some people image that Christianity is, of all things, escapism!) If we attain to such sincerity, two remarkable consequences follow. We enter into the wonderful fellowship of the redeemed. In the Church, we ought all to be absolutely transparent to one another. Fear and a guilty conscience hold far too many of us back, and so the fellowship of the Church is very different from what God would have it be. Secondly, in that fellowship, the blood of Christ is continually available to cleanse us from our faults. We do not become perfect all in a moment. There are faults and failures and blindness, for which forgiveness is needed. For this the blood of Christ—the love shown in his death and the power shown in his resurrection—is available, until God has perfected the work that he wants to do in us.

Prayer *O thou who dwellest in light unapproachable, teach us to rejoice in the light and to walk in the light, until we come to behold thine everlasting light in thy heavenly kingdom; for Jesus' sake.* Amen.

1 John 3, vv. 1 to 12 (3, vv. 1 to 24)

The false teachers, whom St John had to oppose, seem to have been taught an early form of Gnosticism (from the Greek *gnosis*, knowledge.) The characteristics of all these many sects was that they taught that salvation could come through secret and occult knowledge. What holds man in the lower world of darkness and decay is ignorance; by secret knowledge he can be lifted up into the world of light and pure spirit where God is. This idea of knowledge as deliverance always has an attraction for certain types of men; various forms of Eastern wisdom—Buddhism, Vedanta, etc.—are popular in the West at present, and it is notable that they all deny or evade the problem of sin.

St John answers the Gnostics by presenting the true knowledge; the words 'we know' and 'ye know' occur seven times in this chapter alone. But this is not the esoteric knowledge of a mystery; it is the very practical knowledge of a Person. The Christian who knows God is not lifted out of the rough and tumble of ordinary life. On the contrary God is very much interested in that rough and tumble. His aim is to transform the human situation, and to transform his children in it. If a man knows God, his conduct is transformed, so that he does not sin; his relationships are transformed, so that he loves his brother; his purposes are transformed, so that he serves God and not himself.

We do not become children of God by being good. But unless we are good in the most ordinary sense of the term, there is very strong reason for doubting whether we have ever become children of God.

Further work   *Make a list of all the things about which it is said in 1 John that 'we know,' or 'ye know.'*

1 John 4, vv. 7 to 21 (4, vv. 1 to 21)

Here we are at the very heart of the Bible revelation: 'God is Love.'
This love of God is patient, gentle, uncoercive, undemanding. Such
love always involves the willingness to suffer—from the unworthiness
of the one who is loved, from his refusal to accept the offered love
and to respond to it. That is why God suffers for the sins of man.

It is important to note the true translation in v. 19 'we love' (not
'we love him') 'because he first loved us.' All human love is an over-
flow from the love of God. Human love is often blind, selfish and
demanding. But even so, it is the highest thing we know, and we all
know it. In preaching the Gospel to the very simplest peoples in the
world, we can start from the idea of love, because they all know what
it means. But what men need most to know in this troubled modern
world is that, prior to all human love, each one of us is the object of
the unchanging and perfect love of God.

This is also our hope for the future. Here we cannot love God as we
ought to and as we would like to do. Since we are creatures and sinful
we shall never be able to love him as he has loved us. But, if we really
see the love of Christ (v. 10) and understand something of its meaning,
we begin to love him; and 'in heaven' we shall be able to love him to
the fulness of our capacity and as he deserves.

For meditation   *'Now abideth faith, hope, love, these three, and the greatest of these is
love' (1 Corinthians 13, v. 13).*

John 1, vv. 1 to 18 (1, vv. 1 to 51)

We have looked already at the Fourth Gospel as part of the history of Jesus Christ; now we must look at it again as a most important part of the interpretation of that history.

'In the beginning.' The writer deliberately links his book to the first words of Genesis; he is going to set forth the historical event of Jesus Christ in the light of the eternal purpose of God.

'The Word', the *logos*. Many large books have been written about this difficult phrase. We shall find it easiest to understand, if we think in terms of *revelation*. God is a God who reveals himself, who loves to show himself to men. How has he shown himself?

v. 3. 'All thing were made by him.' The creation is the visible word of God. 'The heavens declare the glory of God' (Psalm 19:1). In the universe the power and wisdom of God are revealed.

v. 4. 'The life was the light of men.' God has given to men intelligence and the power to ask questions. There is no race of men on earth which has not some idea of God. Every man has, however dimly, the sense of right and wrong. In conscience God does speak with men.

v. 6. 'There came a man, sent from God.' In the prophets God made himself known through the spoken word. Many refused to listen, but within the Chosen People a true 'people of God' was being called into being.

v. 14. 'The Word became flesh.' We could not perfectly know God, unless God was pleased to become one of us; and this is what God did. A law can never cover all possible cases. A doctrine is never more than an abstraction from life. A life is inexhaustible. The more we study Jesus and ponder the meaning of his life, the more we find there is to learn. It is for this reason that we claim that he is the final revelation of God, and that nothing can be added to this truth.

Prayer *O Word made flesh, true light of men, invisible glory made visible, give us grace humbly to believe and to accept thee, that through thee we may be made the children of God.* Amen.

John 12, vv. 36 to 50 (12, vv. 1 to 50)

The highly artistic structure of the Fourth Gospel presents the life of Jesus in the form of the conflict between faith and unbelief. In 1–10, we see the development of faith and unbelief, and their gradual separation from one another. In 13–19, we see the triumph of unbelief and the eclipse of faith. In 20–21, we see the triumph of faith through the resurrection. Chapter 12 is as it were a pause between the two great sections of the Gospel.

vv. 44–50 is not so much one speech given by Jesus on one occasion as a summary of all the teaching that he has given in the Gospel. Here are all the great pairs of opposites on which the argument has been built up—faith and unbelief; light and darkness; judgment and salvation; life and death.

There is a three-fold challenge in this passage:

1. The total identity in will and purpose between God the Father and Jesus Christ whom he has sent; so that to reject Jesus is also to reject the Father.

2. A decision has to be made and once made it must be publicly confessed, at whatever cost.

3. Judgment is not an arbitrary sentence pronounced by God; it is the sentence that men are pronouncing on themselves all the time by their attitude to 'the Word', to the truth that is offered to them in Jesus. 'The last day' cannot do more than make manifest and permanent the sentence that men have already passed upon themselves.

Men do not like these drastic opposites of the Fourth Gospel. But is anything gained by making the Gospel out to be easier than it is?

To think over *What are your impressions of the conflict between faith and unbelief in the twentieth century?*

John 17, vv. 1 to 26

In all the Bible there are no words more profound than those of this chapter. Jesus, our High Priest, is praying to his Father for us; not for the world as a whole (v. 9), but for his chosen ones (vv. 9 and 20), for those who are to carry on his work to the end of time, to be in the world what Jesus was when he was visibly present with us here.

The key-word of the prayer is *glory*. We usually think of glory as meaning brightness, and so it does; but especially in this Gospel it means far more than that. It means likeness to the Father, oneness of will with the Father, receiving the love of the Father and reflecting it back to him. And here we can see the whole circle—how glory comes back to glory.

1. There is first the eternal glory of the Son, which he had before the world was (v. 5).

2. Then there is the glory which the Son made manifest to men, in the days when he lived among men as a man (vv. 6–8). Because the world is sinful, that glory could be manifested only under the form of suffering.

3. There is the glory which the Son has given to his people in order that they may manifest it to the world (v. 22). This too can be manifest only through suffering (v. 14).

4. And then there is the final glory to which Jesus is leading his people (v. 24), where love alone is triumphant beyond suffering and separation.

There, in a word, is our vocation. We are the glory of Christ (2 Corinthians 8:23). Through us he is to be made known to men, and he can be made known only through love, through suffering and through unity (vv. 22–23). The divisions of the Church are the scandal of the world; we show only broken shafts and fragments of light, instead of the steady glow in which the glory of Christ can be truly seen. What do we propose to do about it?

Prayer *Lord, grant that we who eat of the one Bread and drink of the one Cup may be brought out of division, strife and disunion, not for our own sakes but that thy glory may be seen and that the world may believe in him whom thou hast sent, thy Son Jesus Christ our Lord. Amen.*

Revelation 1, vv. 4 to 20 (1, v. 1 to 3, v. 22)

So at the end we come back to the Book of Revelation at which we have already taken a glance in the Introduction. For a moment the veil is taken away, and the glory of the Risen Lord is seen. 'All authority hath been given unto me in heaven and on earth' (Matthew 28:18) was the word that had been given to the disciples. Now, in time of persecution, when it did not look at all as though Jesus reigned, the word is confirmed to the seer in this tremendous vision.

Once again, the 'Fear not' of the Bible, the word that had been so often on the lips of the human Jesus himself, rings out. It does not mean here just 'Do not be afraid of me'. It means 'Do not be afraid of anything, even of persecution, since nothing can deny the resurrection and the power of him who died and lives'.

The risen Jesus is seen walking in the midst of the Churches—seven of them, the number of completion. They are his Churches, and he cares for them. These are real messages to each Church in times of distress. But in a wonderful way they represent different types of Church, and different periods in the history of the Church; and so the messages have universal significance. The Lord is in the midst of the Churches. Where there is anything good, he praises it. Where there is weakness he probes it to the very heart. He warns. He offers the possibility of renewal. He promises reward for faithfulness unto death. This is the work that he will be doing unto the end of the world. And since you and I are parts of the Church, we too are the objects of his particular and loving care.

Prayer *O thou who walkest in the midst of the Churches and knowest their works, cleanse and renew thy Churches today, that by their witness the nations of the world may be gathered unto thee, who livest and reignest with the Father and the Holy Spirit, one God for ever and ever.* Amen.

Revelation 7, vv. 9 to 17 (7, vv. 1 to 17)

The Revelation is the book of the conflict of God—the conflict of God with all the evil, seen and unseen, in the world; and, since it is through the Church that the purposes of God go forward, the Church must necessarily be engaged in that conflict until all evil is finally destroyed.

1. Already we see the vision of the world-wide Church. There is still a special part to be played by Israel (vv. 1–8); but the 'great multitude' is from all nations and peoples. It is the great unity into which all men are being led in Christ.

2. Tribulation (v. 14) is the mark of this Church—inevitably since its laws are not those of the world. This book was written in time of persecution; it is the expression of the perplexities and sufferings of a martyr church.

3. But this is 'tribulation' for the sake of the Lamb. This is our writer's favourite name for Jesus; it speaks to him of innocence and of innocent suffering. When his people suffer for him, they are brought into more intimate fellowship with him than could be theirs in any other way.

4. Tribulation is not the end—it leads out into triumph. The seven triumph-songs of the book, with their repeated 'Alleluias', have passed into the worship and the hymns of all the Churches.

5. But this is not an impersonal beatitude. It is still the Lamb who leads. The fellowship, begun here, tested and deepened through suffering, will find its fruition and its perfection in that land where nothing can ever change.

And, in the infinite mercy and goodness of God, you and I will be there.

For further study   *Collect and meditate on all the passages in Revelation in which Jesus is spoken of as the Lamb.*

So we have come to the end of the course. Often while writing these notes, I have wondered whether I should ever get to the end of writing them; and perhaps you have wondered whether you would ever get to the end of reading them. But, if we have both stuck to it, here we are at the end. And today it will perhaps be better not to read anything fresh, but to look back over the way travelled. If you can spare as much as half an hour, sit back quietly and think over what you have learned in this journey from Genesis to Revelation.

Then, again if you have time, write down, in not more than five lines for each, answers to the following questions:

1. What do you now believe God to be like?

2. What is your relationship to Jesus Christ?

3. How do you think that your life ought to be lived?

4. What do you now look for in the fellowship of the Church?

5. What is the hope for the future to which you look forward?

If you can do this, it will perhaps help you more than anything else to get clear in your own mind what you have gained in this attempt at 'Seeing the Bible Whole'.

Almighty God, give us grace to be not only hearers but doers of thy Holy Word, not only to admire but to obey thy doctrine, not only to confess but to practise thy religion, not only to love but to live thy Gospel. So grant that what we learn of thy truth we may receive in our hearts and show forth in our lives, to thy glory, through Jesus Christ our Lord.

Amen.

From the Litany:

That it may please thee to bless and keep all thy people;

That it may please thee to give us an heart to love and dread thee, and diligently to live after thy commandments;

That it may please thee to give to all thy people increase of grace to hear meekly thy Word, and to receive it with pure affection, and to bring forth the fruits of the Spirit;

That it may please thee to give us true repentance; to forgive us all our sins, negligences, and ignorances; and to endue us with the grace of thy Holy Spirit to amend our lives according to thy Holy Word;

We beseech thee to hear us, Good Lord.

A Blessing from the Dead Sea Scrolls (1st century BC)

May the Lord bless you with all good and keep you from all evil;

May he give light to your heart with loving wisdom, and be gracious to you with eternal knowledge;

May he lift up his loving countenance upon you for eternal peace.

Amen.

Genesis
1:1—2:4	10
1:31	11
2:5—3:24	11
4:1-15	11
9:8-17	37
11:27—12:9	39
15:1	74
19	26
22:1-19	31, 40
23	43
27	47
28:1-22	41
37—50	42
45:1—46:7	42
50:1-26	43

Exodus
2:23—3:22	44
13:2, 13	40
13:17—15:21	45
19:1—20:21	46
40:38	108

Leviticus
18:21	40

Numbers
22:1—24:25	47
23:5-24	47

Deuteronomy 59
6:1-25	59
6:5	40
22:6-7	60
24:10-22	60

Joshua
3:1—4:24	48
7:24-26	60

Judges 38
4:1—5:31	49
5	3

1 Samuel
9:1—10:16	51
17:1-54	52
19:18-24	21
26:19	41
28	51
31	51

2 Samuel
1:19	51
11:1—18:33	53

1 Kings
8:10-11	108

10:1-29	54
17:1—18:46	55
21:1-29	56

2 Kings 38
5:1-29	57
6:16	25
14:6	60
21:6	40
22:1—23:25	58

1 Chronicles 15

2 Chronicles 15
26:15	27

Ezra 70
3:1—4:6	72

Nehemiah 15, 70
4:1-23	75

Job 77
1:1—3:26	84
5:1-27	85
13:21	26
38—39	86
42:1-17	87

Psalms 15, 77
8	146
16	79
18:7-15	46
19:1	153
29:9	83
50:1-23	80
51:1-17	81
58:1-2	41
72:1-19	82
95:4	10
103:1-22	83
114	48
115:17	79
137:1-9	63
139:7-12	41
145:15	86

Proverbs 78
8:1-36	88

Isaiah 15, 23
1:1-20	26
6:1-13	27
6	44
10:5-11	24
22:1-25	28
30:15	23
33:1-24	29

35:5	98
36:1-22	24
37:1-38	25
40:1-31	67
40—55	66, 92
40—66	66
44:1-28	68
49:1-6	69
49:6	66
50:4-9	69
52:1-9	69
52:13—53:12	69
53	128
54:9	37
61:1	98

Jeremiah 15, 33
1:1-19	44
5:1-31	35
7:4	35
8:11	35
12:3	33
20:1-18	36
31—33	37
52:1-30	34

Lamentations 34

Ezekiel 15, 62
33:1-33	64
37:1-28	65

Daniel 15, 71
7:1-28	76

Hosea 15, 18, 55, 81
1:1—3:5	22
11:1-4	22

Amos 15-18, 55
1:1—3:15	19
3:8	36
5:1-27	20
7:1-17	21
7:7-9	16

Micah 15, 30
3:12	30
6:1-16	31

Nahum 30
1:15—3:19	32
3:8-10	30

Habakkuk
3:3-15	46

Haggai 15, 70
1:1—2:9	73
2:9	70

Zechariah	15, 70
8:1-23	74
9:10	82
Malachi	15

Matthew	91
5:1-48	104
6:1-34	105
6:29	54
6:33	94
7:13-29	106
8:10	57
11:1-25	98
11:5	92
13:1-23	99
18:21-35	102
21:1-17	110
21:23-46	111
22:15-46	112
28:16-20	122
28:18	156

Mark	91
2:1-12	95
3:33-35	146
5:1-20	96
6:5	95
8:27-38	107
9:1-29	108
14:1-31	113
14:24	37
14:32-72	117
14:34	36
14:62	108
15:1-20	118
15:21-41	119

Luke	91
2:1-40	92
2:40-52	93
3:21-22	94
4:1-15	94
7:1-17	97
10:25-37	100
15:1-32	101
19:1-10	109
23:8	95
24:1-49	121
24:50-53	122

John	91, 124, 144
1:1-51	153
1:51	41
2:19-21	108
4:9	70
7:46	111
12:1-50	154
12:28	108
13:7	86
14:1-31	114

14	115
15:1-27	115
16:1-33	116
17:1-26	155
20:1-23	120

Acts	121, 124f.
2:1-21	126
2:22-47	127
2:25ff.	79
7:58	129
8:1	129
8:26-40	128
8:35	69
9:1-31	129
13:35	79
14:23	131
17:1-34	130
24:25	35
28:1-31	131

Romans	124
3:29	67
5—8	139
6:1-23	138
6:4	120
8:1-39	139
8:28	34
8:32	40
15:4	5

1 Corinthians	124
1:28—2:5	133
1:30	88
2:2	130
9:16	36
10:2	45
12:1-31	134
13:1-13	135
13:13	152
15:1-58	136
15:20-28	11
15:28	29
15:50-58	136

2 Corinthians	124
5:1-21	137
8:23	155
11:24-30	132

Galatians	90, 123
2:16	145
3:29	39

Ephesians	124
1:10	143
3:1-21	142
4:1-32	143

Philippians	124
1:9-11	142
2:1-18	140
2:9	19
4:2-3	140

Colossians	124
1:9-12	142

1 & 2 Thessalonians	
	90, 124

1 Timothy	124

2 Timothy	124
2:12-13	46

Titus	124

Philemon	124, 141

Hebrews	
	123f., 144, 146
1:1-2	60
1:1—2:17	146
4:14-16	146
4:15	94
5:7-10	146
11:1-40	147
11:8-10	39
11:40	4
13:14	63

James	90, 124, 144
2:1-26	145

1 Peter	90, 124, 144
1:1-25	148
1:8	92
4:1-19	149
4:17	19

2 Peter	3, 124

1-3 John	91, 124

1 John	144
1:1—2:6	150
3:1-24	151
4:1-21	152

Revelation	
	91, 124, 144
1:1—3:22	156
1:17	74
7:1-17	157
11:8	26
21:1-27	12
22:1-21	13

Ecclesiasticus	78
1-2 Maccabees	15, 71

Dead Sea Scrolls	159
Epistle of Barnabas	
	124
Ignatius:	
Romans 3:3	73

One Increasing Purpose

LENTEN MEDITATIONS

by Stephen Neill

'Many members of the Bible Reading Fellowship have profited from the Bishop's *Seeing the Bible Whole*. This is by way of being a parallel volume to that.

'The readings will serve not only as a guide for their readers during Lent, but as something of an introduction to an understanding of the Bible and its dominant themes.'

Dr Donald Coggan, in Foreword

The selections have been arranged more or less in the order in which they are found in the English Bible.

The readings cover the period from Septuagesima (Third Sunday before Lent) till Easter Day; but they form an invaluable course which may be used at any time.

Send for latest order-form from BRF.

Something Overheard

AN INTRODUCTION TO THE NEW TESTAMENT

by A. E. Harvey

An invaluable setting of the writings against their background of life and witness in the early Christian churches.

Chapters include: 'Overhearing a Conversation', 'Christians at Prayer', 'Preaching and Response', 'According to the Scriptures', 'The Church under Attack', 'The Emergence of the Gospels', 'The Conversation Continues.'

A. E. Harvey is a distinguished Oxford scholar with a great reputation as a teacher and lecturer, speaking with exceptional knowledge, insight and authority. He has written several books, of which *Companion to the New Testament, New English Bible* (OUP) is the best known.

Send for latest order-form from BRF.

THE BIBLE READING FELLOWSHIP

BRF encourages regular informed Bible-reading as a means of renewal in the churches.

BRF publishes daily readings, with explanatory notes in four sets, for all ages:

Series A   For adults with some knowledge of the Bible
Series B   For adults who are beginning daily Bible-reading or who want a small booklet with the Bible passages printed, a devotional commentary and prayers
Compass   For junior children, with illustrations and activities
Discovery   For young adults who want to include the Bible in their search for meaning and identity.

Groups of BRF members all over the world meet to discuss the readings.

Members may join at any time.

BRF also publishes introductory booklets on Bible-reading, group study guides, children's aids, audio-visual material, etc.

Write for details

St Michael's House 2 Elizabeth St London SW1

P.O. Box M Winter Park Florida 32790 U.S.A.

Jamieson House Constitution Ave Reid ACT 2601 Australia

The BRF Prayer

O God our Father,
who in the Holy Scriptures
hast given us thy Word
to be our teacher and guide:

Help us and all the members of our Fellowship
to seek in our daily reading
the guidance of thy Holy Spirit,

That we may learn more of thee
and of thy will for us,
and so grow in likeness to thy Son,
Jesus Christ our Lord.

Cover Picture

Bible theme: Water
Tapestry at Regina Pacis Priory, Cockfosters, London

Reproduced by kind permission. Photograph by John Ray.